# WILD ANIMALS OF SINGAPORE

A Photographic Guide to
Mammals, Reptiles, Amphibians
and Freshwater Fishes

**Project Co-ordinators**
Nick Baker and Kelvin K. P. Lim

**Contributors**
Nick Baker, Chan Kwok Wai, Cheryl Chia, Vilma D'Rozario,
Kelvin K.P. Lim, Norman T-L. Lim, Leong Tzi Ming, Celine Low,
Tony O'Dempsey, Timothy Pwee, Subaraj Rajathurai,
Robert C. H. Teo and Yeo Suay Hwee

First published in 2008 by Draco Publishing and
Distribution Pte. Ltd. and Nature Society (Singapore)

Copyright © 2008 Draco Publishing and Distribution
Pte Ltd and Nature Society (Singapore)
Copyright © 2008 in photographs: with individual
photographers as per credits
ISBN: 978-981-05-9459-6

Draco Publishing and Distribution Pte. Ltd.
29 Transit Road #04-13
Singapore 778905
Website: www.dracopublishing.com
E-mail: msnbc@singnet.com.sg

Nature Society (Singapore)
510 Geylang Road
#02-05 The Sunflower
Singapore 389446

Compiled by Vertebrate Study Group
(see page 174-175 for details)
Co-ordination and text: Nick Baker and Kelvin Lim
Editing: Nick Baker, Kelvin Lim and Morten Strange
Photo consultants: Chan Kwok Wai and Norman Lim
Line drawings: Kelvin Lim
Map: Tony O'Dempsey
Graphic design: Leng Soo-Tsu
Project Director: Ng Bee Choo
Printed in Singapore by Utopia Press Pte Ltd

Front cover: (Clockwise from top left) Common Palm
Civet photo by Norman Lim; Oriental Whip Snake
photo by Chan Kwok Wai; Asian Climbing Perch photo
by Tan Heok Hui; Four-ridged Toad photo by Chan
Kwok Wai.

Back cover: Top photo by Nick Baker; Bottom row
photo by Kelvin Lim.

Page 7 photo by Tan Heok Hui.

**WILD ANIMALS OF SINGAPORE**

# CONTENTS

# SPONSOR'S MESSAGE

**Chris Gibson-Robinson**
VP Operations & New
Ventures (Southeast Asia)
Aabar Petroleum
Investments Company PJSC

Singapore is a small island that has been heavily urbanised and largely deforested. However, thanks to forward thinking by the Singapore government, there are tracts of preserved forest, mangrove and parklands in which a diverse fauna and flora survive and thrive.

The Nature Society (Singapore) (NSS) is dedicated to the study, conservation and enjoyment of the natural heritage of Singapore and beyond. The Vertebrate Study Group of the NSS and its many volunteers regularly conduct surveys of these last remaining natural habitats to record the numbers and species diversity of backboned animals that include fish, amphibians, reptiles and mammals.

As described in the Guide a number of species are at critically low numbers such as the tiny Lesser Mousedeer, the Banded Leaf Monkey and the Slow Loris. The introduction of alien species has resulted in the reduction of native species of freshwater fish, for example.

We at Aabar believe it is of vital importance that society does its utmost to preserve and improve our natural heritage. We seek to minimise the impact of our business on the areas in which we work by conducting our activities in an environmentally and socially responsible manner.

We hope that this book, with its informative text and superb pictures, will inspire others in Singapore to help NSS preserve the wildlife and the environment, and take an active interest in the vertebrates that can be seen with a little patience in Singapore's parks and nature reserves.

We are delighted to support publication of this important Guide.

The Cream-coloured Giant Squirrel (*Ratufa affinis*) is one of those animals that might have been lost in the process of Singapore's development.
Morten Strange (Pasoh Forest Reserve, Malaysia)

# FOREWORD

**The Earl of Cranbrook**
MA, PhD, DSc (Hon), DL,
JBS (Hon), PNBS (Hon)

Towards the end of July 1956, a small cargo vessel of the Blue Funnel line, 28 days out of Liverpool, finally dropped anchor in the Singapore Roads. Eager "bumboats" clustered round, took aboard the eight passengers and rowed us to Collyer Quay. Thus and there did I first set foot on Singapore Island. Would that a book such as this had existed then! Yet, had the job been done, over the subsequent half-century I would have missed the many delights of the shared effort, along with fellow field workers and observers, colleagues, students and others, who have progressively charted the rich animal life of this tropical region. The information gathered in these pages, by the latest dedicated team of investigators and skilled photographers, is a landmark contribution to the regional literature, and a lasting credit to the contributors and compilers.

Biogeographically, Singapore and its islands form a small, distinctive subregional entity, until a few thousand years ago attached to the Malay Peninsula and, earlier, part of the great Sunda subcontinent exposed by lowered sea-levels during a long period of global cooling (the last "Ice Age"). Thus the original vertebrate fauna was closely related to that of southern Peninsular Malaysia. This indigenous assemblage was slightly modified by the natural event of isolation. Subsequently, as related in the Introduction, animal life has been severely altered by human intervention. Little is known of the early people whose city walls

were still standing in January 1819, when Stamford Raffles planted the British flag within their precincts. Much greater detail is available documenting the rapid land clearance and settlement that followed in the 19th century, and the huge expansion of residential, commercial and industrial development in the 20th. This book records some distinctive animal species that have been lost in the process. But it is heartening to learn from these pages how many truly indigenous animals are still found in the mix of available habitats on Singapore and its islands. It is also intriguing to read of the variety of introductions, many inadvertent, that now augment the natural richness of animal life in the territory of the Republic.

Singapore today is a cosmopolitan state, crowded with foreign visitors and populated by citizens with an international outlook. For many people, urban life, with its conveniences and constraints, is reality. But, as the contributors to this delightful book show so well, it needs no great effort to step aside and discover the truly real world of nature. With this guide, it should be possible to identify the wide diversity of wild animals to be found in different habitats, urban, rural and coastal. The authors' diligence is such that, if you can't name one of your finds, it may be a new record! Look well and, if you are in Singapore, enjoy the natural world; if you are not, revel in this presentation of the animal life you are missing.

**Banded Leaf Monkey
(*Presbytis femoralis*)**
Daniel Koh

# PREFACE

NATURE SOCIETY
SINGAPORE

**Vertebrate
Study Group**

The Vertebrate Study Group (VSG), one of the key special interest groups of the Nature Society (Singapore), has compiled this pocket guide with the aim of furthering the appreciation of Singapore's lesser known wildlife by the general public. Singapore's birdlife is well documented, and many guide books are available on the subject. However, for the vertebrate groups covered here, namely freshwater fishes, amphibians, terrestrial reptiles and terrestrial mammals, previous publications lack the extensive in-situ images used in this book.

The last twenty years has seen a significant increase in our understanding of the diversity, distribution and habits of Singapore's vertebrates. This is a result of detailed vertebrate surveys and the compilation and sharing of sighting records by the VSG, National Parks Board (NParks) and National University of Singapore (NUS).

New sightings of interesting vertebrates in Singapore should be submitted using the Sightings Form available on www.ecologya-sia.com operated by Nick Baker.

Every photograph in this book was taken in Singapore by amateur photographers with a deep interest in our local fauna. Every photo, that is, except that of the Cream-coloured Giant Squirrel on page 6;

The opportunity to capture a local image of this beautiful creature may have passed into history. All images were taken in or adjacent to the animal's natural habitats, and captive settings have been avoided. The majority of pictures were taken in the last three years, using modern digital cameras. The sophistication of today's camera systems has contributed to many good quality images.

Included in this book is a fully revised checklist of the freshwater fishes, amphibians, terrestrial reptiles and terrestrial mammals of Singapore. This timely revision follows a thorough review of the status of all species, whether common or rare, widely distributed or restricted in range, native or introduced, etc. Species not seen for 50 years have been listed as locally extinct, but many recent finds have been added.

The VSG is indebted to those who are prepared to routinely forsake their comfortable homes, to spend their time in the heat and humidity, getting sweaty, hot and thirsty in the quiet documentation and photography of these diverse creatures. Fortunately the general public can now take advantage of an increased network of trails and boardwalks in our nature reserves to explore these wonders of nature with greater ease. We hope this small book will add to your enjoyment.

# INTRODUCTION

SINGAPORE'S equatorial location and humid, tropical climate places the country in the heart of one of the world's biodiversity hotspots. Though isolated since the end of the last Ice Age, around 10,000 years ago, it still retains a fauna and flora which has much in common with the southern parts of Peninsular Malaysia.

Geologically the country is underlain by a granite core of Triassic age (about 200 million years old), which is overlain by later Triassic sediments and recent alluvium. Granite hills dominate the central part of Singapore Island and Pulau Ubin, while smaller sandstone hills are to be found in the south of Singapore Island. There are also significant areas of reclaimed land.

The original habitat of the main island of Singapore, and of its larger offshore islands, would have mainly comprised coastal hill forest, dominated by rainforest trees. Remnants of this habitat still survive in the Bukit Timah and Central Catchment nature reserves. Scattered patches of freshwater swamp forest would have dominated low-lying inland areas, and the coastline would have been extensively fringed by mangrove.

Large-scale habitat destruction occurred in the 19th century. Forests were felled, agricultural areas and rubber plantations established and more land was converted to urban use to house a growing, migrant population. This process continued into the 20th century, in the latter half of which there was widespread conversion of rural areas, once dominated by simple kampungs (villages) and small-scale farms, into large public housing estates built by the Housing Development Board (HDB).

Now, at the start of the 21st century, only a small percentage of Singapore's terrestrial habitats can be considered as primary, largely untouched by the hand of man. Such areas include the primary rainforest of Bukit Timah Nature Reserve and isolated patches of primary rainforest and freshwater swamp forest in the Central Catchment Nature Reserve.

Singapore's northern islands also have a chequered history of exploitation and a slow process of regeneration. Pulau Ubin was once extensively cleared for kampungs, rubber plantations and granite extraction. Today, the island is largely given over to outward bound activities and recreation. It remains a charming place to visit and has its own remnant wildlife to discover. Pulau Tekong, currently off-limits to the public, was also once dominated by rubber plantations and kampungs but is slowly reverting back to more natural habitat. Both islands harbour some of Singapore's best remaining mangroves - the Sungei Besar inlet on Pulau Ubin, and the northern mangrove areas of Pulau Tekong. Both islands, however, lack a remnant stand of primary rainforest from which flora and fauna can repopulate the secondary growth.

The Southern Islands comprise a few larger islands, such as Sentosa and the live-firing areas of Pulau Sudong, Pulau Pawai and Pulau Senang, and numerous smaller islets. Their coastal and intertidal habitats remain key refuges for marine fauna and flora.

The highest vertebrate diversity is found in primary rainforest and freshwater swamp forest. Secondary forest adjacent to such habitats may also have a relatively high level of diversity, but secondary forest which is fragmented and not contiguous with primary habitats will generally have lower diversity. In rural areas, public parks and gardens diversity is lower, but there is still much to see. In the tropics, one only has to sit at home as night falls to observe the local wildlife : house-dwelling geckos epitomise nature's strength at adaptation.

Thus, Singapore's land vertebrate diversity (i.e. those species covered in this book) is impressive for a small, highly urbanised nation: At least 35 species of native freshwater fish, 25 species of amphibian, over 90 species of reptile, and at least 50 species of mammal still exist.

### Definitions

In this book, the term "vertebrates" refers to mammals, reptiles, amphibians and fishes, but not birds. "Non-avian vertebrates" is probably more accurate, but is clumsy to use repeatedly in the text, and is, therefore, avoided.

This book covers vertebrate species that are freshwater, semi-terrestrial, terrestrial and aerial in habits. Fishes described here are restricted to those that complete their life-cycles in freshwater beyond tidal influence. Fully aquatic species of reptiles and amphibians are included if these are found in freshwater. We also include aquatic snakes of coastal marine habitats that deliberately emerge onto land from time to time. Vertebrates that live their entire lives in saltwater, such as estuarine and marine fishes, sea turtles, sea-snakes, dolphins, whales and the dugong are not covered in this book.

With regard to the terms "fish" and "fishes", the word "fish" is used when describing a single specimen or many specimens of the same species, while "Fishes" should properly be used when discussing more than one species.

## Habitats

Only a minority of vertebrates are able to adapt to significant habitat changes. The vast majority of species are inextricably bound by dietary or reproductive requirements to the habitat and niche they have evolved to fill. An understanding of habitat type will, therefore, lead to an understanding of the vertebrate species likely to be found there.

### Primary Rainforest

This is native forest which has been largely undisturbed by the direct hand of man, i.e. it has not been logged or cleared. It is dominated by a high canopy, with huge Dipterocarps reaching 50 metres or more, with straight trunks and buttressed roots.

Dispersed amongst these forest giants and other large trees are figs, rattans, lianas, palms, ferns and other flora. This abundance of plant life keeps the forest floor in near-permanent shade. Only 2% of sunlight reaches the ground, except where tree-falls have opened a gap in the canopy. Forest vertebrates have evolved to fill every niche in this complex ecosystem, and diversity is high. In Singapore, primary rainforest still remains at Bukit Timah Nature Reserve and in isolated parts of the Central Catchment Nature Reserve.

Chan Kwok Wai

**Primary forest**

### Secondary Forest

In secondary forest the original forest has been exploited, either partially or fully, mainly through timber extraction. In Singapore this category of habitat includes young and mature secondary forest and abandoned rubber plantations with significant secondary growth. Vertebrate diversity ranges from fair in young secondary to highly diverse in

Nick Baker

**Secondary forest**

mature secondary. Under the slow process of succession all types of secondary forest should eventually revert to primary rainforest, but this may take many hundreds of years. If there is no adjacent primary forest to contribute floral and faunal diversity, secondary forest may in fact never reach its original diversity. The Central Catchment Nature Reserve is Singapore's most extensive area of mainly secondary forest.

## Freshwater Swamp Forest

Low-lying forest areas are characterised by waterlogged soil, networks of small, acidic streams and a unique flora and fauna adapted to such conditions. Vertebrate diversity is high, with many species able to survive only in this habitat, particularly amphibians and freshwater fishes. Freshwater swamp forest occurs in parts of the Central Catchment Nature Reserve.

Freshwater swamp

Freshwater ponds

## Scrubland and Grassland

Abandoned, cleared land which once supported small-scale farms and kampungs quickly turns into a patchwork of lallang grassland, low scrub and isolated areas of secondary woodland with fruit trees such as Jackfruit, Rambutan, Mango and Durian, and fast growing trees such as *Casuarina*, and the introduced species of *Acacia* and *Albizia*. On Singapore Island these habitats exist in the north-west at Lim Chu Kang, Neo Tiew and Kranji. Parts of Pulau Ubin also fit this category.

Scrubland at Neo Tiew

## Parks and Gardens

Singapore has a varied selection of parks, gardens and park connectors. The trees and shrubs in such areas are carefully tended and bear little resemblance to natural habitats, though in some parks magnificent fig trees have somehow survived the conversion from forest to kampung to parkland.

Vertebrate diversity in parks and gardens is generally low. In recent years, however, there has been an encouraging trend towards providing small areas of wildlife habitat in Singapore's public parks.

Parkland and golf course

For example, the "long grass areas" in East Coast Park have now regenerated to a type of secondary forest, and efforts to attract wildlife have been made at the Eco-lake at the Singapore Botanic Gardens. Hopefully the increasing network of park connectors will contribute to an increase in wildlife diversity in public areas.

**Forest stream**

### Aquatic Habitats
Natural aquatic habitats include freshwater swamp and forest streams, both high in diversity. Man-made or converted habitats include rural streams, abandoned fish ponds, concretised drains, ornamental lakes and reservoirs. These generally have lower vertebrate diversity but still provide a haven for local wildlife.

Though Singapore has an average annual rainfall of 2.3 metres, its water consumption is high because of its dense population. A network of reservoirs exists to serve this need for water. There are four large reservoirs in the Central Catchment area which were formed by the damming of low-lying areas, and numerous coastal reservoirs were created when tidal mangrove inlets were dammed. Reservoirs are mainly populated by introduced fish species.

Mosquito control measures have resulted in the concretisation of most natural streams, except for those in the nature reserves. This has had a significant, negative impact on biodiversity, and it is debatable whether this measure is the most effective solution to vector control.

A recent proposal to restore a 2.5 km section of the upper reaches of the Kallang River, where it is no more than a concrete-lined storm drain, to a more natural waterway with newly-created aquatic habitats and to integrate the regenerated river into the popular Bishan Park, is an exciting sign of a more enlightened approach to urban planning. However, it must be recognised that such man-made wildlife habitats lack the complex diversity of undisturbed natural habitats.

### Mangrove
Mangrove habitat comprises intertidal areas, such as mudflats or sandbanks, and abandoned coastal fish and prawn ponds, colonised by tree species such as *Rhizophora*, *Avicennia*, *Bruguiera* and *Sonneratia* which thrive in saline water.

Invertebrate life in the mangrove ecosystem is dominated by crabs, prawns, shellfish and worms. These support a complex food web which allows vertebrates to flourish. Mangrove areas also play a key role as a nursery for marine fish stocks - mature Barramundi (sea bass), for example, will migrate into mangrove to spawn, and the fish fry will remain in the mangrove until they are of sufficient size to venture into open seas.

Large areas of Singapore's mangrove have been lost to industrial development and conversion to coastal reservoirs. However, there are important remnants including, on Singapore Island, the Lim Chu Kang - Sungei Buloh - Mandai Mangrove belt, Sungei Seletar and Sungei Punggol estuaries, and the remnant mangrove at Pasir Ris and Changi Creek. On Pulau Ubin and Pulau Tekong important areas of mangrove still exist, and mangrove still clings to the coast of some of the Southern Islands.

**Mangrove**

### Urban
Although vertebrate diversity is low in urban areas there are some species which manage to survive in such concrete environments. These include two species of rats, House Shrew, various geckos, Common Fruit Bat, and some snakes, including the Reticulated Python which is often captured and removed from housing estates.

### Habitat Fragmentation
Besides habitat loss, habitat fragmentation is a major contributor to any decline in species diversity and abundance. In Singapore, fragmentation is caused by roads, housing and industrial development and conversion of habitat to other uses. Though further habitat fragmentation of Singapore's nature reserves is now less likely, much of the damage has already been done.

Nick Baker

**The Bukit Timah Expressway**

For example, the Bukit Timah Expressway (BKE), constructed in the 1980s, severed the natural connection between the secondary forest of the Central Catchment area and the primary rainforest of Bukit Timah, thus curtailing the potential repopulation of the former area by species from the latter area. The planned faunal link spanning the BKE might mitigate this problem to some extent.

Road widening too is a serious problem. Wildlife, which in the past might have successfully crossed an unlit two-lane road with light traffic, is less likely to cross a well-lit six-lane road with heavy traffic and survive.

In time, with greater understanding of the problem of habitat fragmentation and the will to put things right, these impacts may be partially alleviated. Simple measures include planting park connectors with more dense stands of native tree species, allowing the canopy of wayside trees to connect across roads, thereby allowing arboreal species to move from one fragment to another, and simple tunnels underneath wide roads to provide terrestrial species a safe crossing point. Ultimately, the long-term solution is for natural habitats to be sensitively integrated into urban planning.

# Extinction
In Singapore considerable local extinction of indigenous vertebrate fauna occurred following the large-scale felling of primary rainforest, mainly in the 19th century. Many of the larger mammals such as Tiger, Clouded Leopard, Barking Deer and Sambar Deer disappeared. Currently other mammal species stand on the brink of local extinction, including the beautiful Cream-coloured Giant Squirrel. This large rodent was first described from Singapore by Sir Stamford Raffles himself, but it has not been seen since 1995.

There is still a risk of further extinction of our larger mammals. The long-term survival of the small population of Banded Leaf Monkey in the Central Catchment Nature Reserve is a cause for concern, and other species such as the Sunda Slow Loris and Leopard Cat remain in a precarious position. Reptiles and amphibians seem to have fared somewhat better, though some of the rarer species have not been seen for many years. (We consider a vertebrate species to be locally extinct if it has not been seen for 50 years.)

With global warming, deforestation and other threats to the earth's environment, we are now beginning to understand how mankind's industrial activities can affect even remote corners of the planet. There is scarcely any part of the planet which can now be considered as truly pristine. Singapore will not escape the impact of these global problems, in fact the country now annually suffers significant air pollution from forest fires in neighbouring countries. Preserving Singapore's natural heritage in the face of rising temperatures and rising sea levels will present a major challenge.

The Three-striped Ground Squirrel (*Lariscus insignis*) is a small mammal species that is now extinct in Singapore. These two specimens at the Raffles Museum of Biodiversity Research were collected at Changi in 1912.

# Alien Species

Adding further stress to Singapore's native wildlife is the problem of alien introductions. An increasingly affluent population and a consumerist society has resulted in a significant pet trade: abandoned pets such as iguanas, terrapins, rabbits and many species of freshwater fish are often released into our nature reserves and some now form viable populations. Accidental introductions have also occurred - reptiles in particular are easy stowaways in vehicles or containers coming into Singapore. An example is the Changeable Lizard, first seen in Singapore in the early 1980s. This species, a native of northern Peninsular Malaysia and Thailand, has now become so common that it can be seen throughout Singapore Island. In recent years, the White-spotted Slug Snake, again from northern Peninsular Malaysia, has been encountered in Singapore a number of times. It is not clear how it arrived on these shores.

Alien introductions are to be strongly discouraged. Introduced species can out-compete local species for food, territory or other resources, thereby driving local species to extinction. In recent years, the National Parks Board and the Nature Society (Singapore) have organised a campaign to discourage the release of captive animals by well-meaning people. Readers of this book are strongly encouraged not to release animals into the wild.

Red-eared terrapins (*Trachemys scripta elegans*) are a North American species, commonly released in Singapore's waterways by pet owners.

The American Bullfrog (*Lithobates catesbeianus*), sold alive in some local restaurants, are often released into Singapore's ponds and streams.

## INTRODUCTION

### HOW TO SPOT WILDLIFE

Overseas visitors to the tropics often have the mistaken belief that wildlife is abundant and easy to find in the forest, while local visitors to Singapore's forests often come away with the opinion that there is nothing to be seen, apart from a few monkeys. The truth lies somewhere in between. In tropical forests, wildlife, including vertebrates, is highly diverse but not necessarily abundant. Most species have evolved to be quiet, secretive and well camouflaged. In order to locate these elusive creatures one needs to be patient, have sharp eyes and walk slowly and quietly. A pair of binoculars will help considerably in spotting lizards on tree trunks, locating primates and squirrels in the canopy, or scanning the path ahead for snakes. Keeping an ear open for unusual sounds is important too.

Different vertebrate groups prefer different weather conditions. Many reptiles like hot, sunny days. Amphibians tend to prefer damp, rainy nights. Mammals are either nocturnal, or are only active in the early morning or late afternoon (i.e. crepuscular). Some species prefer to sun themselves, others to stay cool in the forest. Above all, wildlife prefers to be undisturbed so ideally one should walk the quieter forest trails. A dose of good luck also helps - some days you will have the luck to find interesting wildlife, but on other days luck may not be with you!

A simple digital camera is generally sufficient for the enthusiast to capture a reasonable image which may later be used to help identify the species.

**Below: Observing a Malayan Water Monitor at Sungei Buloh Wetland Reserve.**

Kelvin Lim

# A Word on Snakes

SNAKES bear the brunt of mankind's fear and ignorance of unfamiliar wildlife. However their reputation is largely unwarranted, particularly in Southeast Asia. In Singapore there are around 70 species of land-dwelling snakes, depending on how they are counted, of which less than one in five is considered highly venomous and another one in five mildly venomous.

Of the venomous species only a minority are considered "aggressive" - meaning that they will bite if disturbed or tormented. This applies to the cobras and pit-vipers. The seemingly docile venomous species, such as coral snakes and kraits, are usually conspicuously coloured so that they can be seen from a distance, and thus, avoided. Most snake encounters are with rather nervous creatures which take the earliest opportunity to flee, or else remain motionless hoping that they remain undetected.

Leong Tzi Ming

**Look at me, I'm dangerous! The Blue Malayan Coral Snake advertises its toxicity with eye-catching colours.**

Cases of snakebite are extremely rare in Singapore. It is no exaggeration to say that the most dangerous part of a trip to a nature reserve is the risk of a road accident while traveling to your destination. The last known case of fatal snakebite in Singapore was in the early 1990s.

For those fearful of snakes, the best approach is to stay on the trail and keep an eye on the path ahead of you. This will reduce the risk of an unexpected encounter. If you should chance upon a snake, there is no reason to be afraid. Simply give the snake a wide berth. As a rule, the larger the snake, the more space you should allow it.

For those who do not fear snakes, we strongly urge you not to pick up or handle any wild snake, even if you are sure that it is non-venomous. Snakes, like all wild animals, do not appreciate being touched, and many will try to bite in self-defence. They should only be admired from a distance.

Snakes tend to act in a defensive manner when approached too closely. If a snake flips over to reveal its boldly patterned and/or brightly coloured underside, do not touch it. If it rears up with the front part of its body compressed (often to reveal brightly coloured skin between the scales), forked tongue protruding, or opening its mouth and hissing, do not go nearer. Instead, gently back away until it calms down. If you encounter a cobra with its hood outstretched, back away slowly to a safe distance. The locally common Equatorial Spitting Cobra can spray venom from its fangs for a distance of one to two metres. It aims the venom at the eyes of its perceived "attacker", which may cause serious damage to the sensitive tissues of the eye if this is not quickly washed away.

Some snakes like pit-vipers tend to remain in the same spot for some days. Often they can be found coiled and unmoving amongst low vegetation. Staying on open trails makes good sense in order to avoid disturbing vegetation where these snakes may lie concealed.

Snakes possess great beauty in their colour and patterning, and superb adaptation to different of modes of life. Take the time to learn to recognise the more common species, and treasure your encounters with these remarkable creatures.

Kelvin Lim

**Please stay on the trail! The Wagler's Pit-viper, like this one at Hindhede Park, can remain for days at one spot, well-camouflaged amongst vegetation.**

# PLACES OF INTEREST

## Nature Reserves

Singapore's National Parks Act (Cap. 198A) and Parks and Trees Act (2005) provide the highest legal protection to four nature reserves:
- Bukit Timah Nature Reserve
- Central Catchment Nature Reserve
- Sungei Buloh Wetland Reserve
- Labrador Nature Reserve

These areas are under the direct management of the National Parks Board (NParks).

### Bukit Timah Nature Reserve

This 163-hectare reserve includes Singapore's largest remaining area of primary rainforest. It is bounded by the Bukit Timah Expressway, Rifle Range Road, Upper Bukit Timah Road, and Dairy Farm Road.

Bukit Timah is Singapore's highest hill at 164 metres above sea level. Often considered the jewel in the crown of Singapore's protected areas, of late the jewel is looking somewhat tarnished. The paths appear a little too well-trodden, tree-falls are common, and landslides and erosion are occurring. The reserve suffers from former quarrying activity, and from being surrounded on nearly all sides by six-lane roads. There is, however, a great diversity of fauna and flora to be enjoyed here.

On the western side of Bukit Timah lies Hindhede Park, an area of mainly secondary forest which has been extensively replanted with native vegetation. To the south, adjacent to Rifle Range Road, lies the Kampong Trail. This once inhabited area has now reverted to secondary forest and makes for an interesting walk.

Try to spot: Long-tailed Macaque, Malayan Colugo, Common Treeshrew, Slender Squirel, Oriental Whip Snake, Red-necked Bronzeback, Wagler's Pit-viper, Brown Tree Skink, Kendall's Rock Gecko, Malesian Frog, Copper-cheeked Frog.

Kelvin Lim

**Bukit Timah Nature Reserve**

*Kelvin Lim*

**Central Catchment Nature Reserve**

## Central Catchment Nature Reserve

This large reserve comprises around 2000 hectares of mainly secondary forest surrounding the Upper Seletar, Upper Peirce, Lower Peirce and MacRitchie Reservoirs. It is bordered by the Bukit Timah Expressway, Pan Island Expressway, Lornie Road, Upper Thomson Road and Mandai Road. While NParks oversees the protection and management of the forests, the Public Utilities Board (PUB) is responsible for the four reservoirs and their respective public parks.

Remnant areas of primary rainforest still exist in the Central Catchment, particularly around MacRitchie Reservoir, and there are localised areas of freshwater swamp forest. Trails and boardwalks are well marked, and at Bukit Kallang there is a canopy walkway which allows for fine views over the forest.

Try to spot: Lesser Mousedeer, Malayan Colugo, Long-tailed Macaque, Slender Squirrel, Twin-barred Gliding Snake, Black-bearded Flying Dragon, Clouded Monitor, Copper-cheeked Frog, Forest Snakehead and various other species of freshwater fish.

*Note: The Bukit Timah Nature Reserve and the Central Catchment Nature Reserve are jointly referred to as the Central Nature Reserves.*

## Sungei Buloh Wetland Reserve

Located in the north-western corner of Singapore Island, this nature reserve comprises abandoned prawn ponds, scrubland, mangrove, mudflats and freshwater ponds. It covers 130 hectares, and adjacent to the reserve is the Kranji Nature Trail.

Primarily protected and managed as mangrove and intertidal habitats for migratory birds, the reserve has a good diversity of other vertebrates, including brackish water

*Kelvin Lim*

**Sungei Buloh Wetland Reserve**

fishes, snakes, larger reptiles and aquatic mammals. The reserve has an excellent network of hides, trails and mangrove boardwalks.

Try to spot: Smooth Otter, Malayan Water Monitor, Estuarine Crocodile, Dog-faced Water Snake, Paradise Gliding Snake, Mangrove Skink.

### Labrador Nature Reserve

Located in the west coast area of Singapore Island this small, 10-hectare reserve exists primarily to protect a small stretch of rocky coastline with coastal forest, sandy shore and associated habitats. At low tide coral reefs are partly exposed.

Try to spot: Plantain Squirrel, Common Fruit Bat, Sumatran Flying Dragon, Mourning Gecko, Common Sun Skink, Asian Toad.

# General Areas

**Pulau Ubin:** This large, boomerang-shaped island off Singapore's north-east coast is well worth a visit for those with a general interest in nature. Once extensively cleared for quarrying, rubber plantations, agriculture and villages, it now comprises mainly secondary forest, and overgrown orchards and plantations. Healthy areas of mangrove still exist on the northern and southern coasts. At its eastern tip lies Chek Jawa, an expanse of diverse intertidal habitats once threatened with destruction by land reclamation, but now conserved for the foreseeable future. The island is partly managed by the National Parks Board as a nature area, and most of the eastern two-thirds of the island is accessible to the public.

Kelvin Lim

**Labrador Nature Reserve**

Try to spot: Wild Boar, Common Palm Civet, Oriental Small-clawed Otter, Equatorial Spitting Cobra, Clouded Monitor and Mangrove Frog.

**Sentosa:** Lying off the south coast of Singapore, Sentosa is marked for tourism and recreation. For those not put off by its commercialism, the island has various habitats to explore including coastal forest, parkland, beaches and rocky cliffs. It is managed by the Sentosa Development Corporation.

Try to spot: Long-tailed Macaque, Plantain Squirrel, Green Crested Lizard.

**Sentosa's coastal forest**

**Changi:** The north-eastern corner of Singapore Island is generally referred to as Changi. Interspersed with developed areas are habitats which include beaches, mangrove, secondary forest, scrubland and parkland.

Try to spot: Common Palm Civet, Plantain Squirrel, Changeable Lizard.

**Reclaimed beach at Changi**

**Southern Islands:** The various islands, rocky islets and submerged reefs lying south of Singapore comprise the Southern Islands. They support remnant coastal and back-beach vegetation, rocky shores, sandy beaches, mangrove and coral reefs. Given the small size of most of these islands, terrestrial vertebrate diversity is generally low, but intertidal and coral reef diversity is high. The islands of Sudong, Pawai and Senang are closed to the general public.

Try to spot: Malayan Water Monitor, Mangrove Skink, Yellow-lipped Sea Krait, other marine reptiles and mammals.

**Neo Tiew:** Between the mangrove belt of Singapore's north-western coast (which includes Sungei Buloh Wetland Reserve) and Kranji Reservoir lies the general area of Neo Tiew. It comprises mainly abandoned traditional farmland, fruit orchards and

**Neo Tiew**

fishponds, although some areas now support more intensive methods of agriculture and farming. There are many small rural streams and, fringing Kranji Reservoir, freshwater marshes. Neo Tiew supports its own diversity of vertebrates including freshwater fishes, open-country snake species, and other wildlife which has adapted to the area. For those who enjoy a walk in the "open countryside" this is one place to go.

Try to spot: Malayan Water Monitor, Striped Keelback, Painted Bronzeback, Changeable Lizard, Dark-sided Chorus Frog, Mozambique Tilapia, Croaking Goramy, Two-spot Goramy, Aruan.

# Parks and Gardens

Singapore has numerous public parks and other green oases, many of which are located in the heart of new towns. Vertebrate diversity in such areas is low to fair but there are, however, four parks which are considered to hold greater interest due to their more diverse wildlife. These are Singapore Botanic Gardens, Bukit Batok Nature Park, Kent Ridge Park and Pasir Ris Park.

**Singapore Botanic Gardens:** Founded in 1859 and located close to the city, this historical park is a botanical treasure trove. Within its boundaries there is a fair diversity of vertebrates including many species of frog. There is also a small, 5-hectare patch of rather degraded primary rainforest. The gardens are protected as a national park under the National Parks Act.

To the west of the gardens is a large private property of around 50 hectares which has largely reverted to secondary forest. Alhough off-limits to the public the edge of the forest can be viewed from Tyersall Avenue.

Try to spot: Slender Squirrel, Oriental Whip Snake, Red-eared Terrapin, Malayan Giant Frog, Common Greenback, Common Tree Frog, Aruan.

**Singapore Botanic Gardens**

**Bukit Batok Nature Park:** Located at the edge of Bukit Batok New Town, this attractive public park was once a granite quarry. The park includes a small quarry lake and an area of secondary forest with a fair diversity of vertebrates. It is bounded on the east and separated from Bukit Timah Nature Reserve by Upper Bukit Timah Road.

Try to spot: Malayan Colugo, Common Treeshrew, Slender Squirrel, Malayan Box Terrapin, Clouded Monitor, Green Crested Lizard.

**Bukit Batok Nature Park**

**Kent Ridge Park:** Kent Ridge is the most significant of Singapore's southern sandstone hills. Once extensively cleared it now supports secondary forest, scrubland and parkland. The ridge extends westwards to the campus of the National University of Singapore. A 300-metre canopy walk not only allows for fine views to the north but is also a good spot to observe the habits of bats at dusk.

Try to spot: Plantain Squirrel, Common Treeshrew, Pouched Tomb Bat, Common Fruit Bat, Oriental Whip Snake, Common Sun Skink.

**Kent Ridge Park canopy walk**

**Pasir Ris Park:** At the eastern end of this popular park lies a small but important area of mangrove, which includes a boardwalk allowing the visitor a close-up view of the habitat. Four species of water snake have been recorded from this area, and the observant visitor may be able to spot the common Dog-faced Water Snake late in the afternoon at low tide.

Try to spot: Dog-faced Water Snake, Mourning Gecko, Banded Bull Frog.

Pasir Ris Park boardwalk

# Restricted Areas

Restricted areas, not accessible to the general public, often harbour significant fauna and flora. Two sizeable military training areas are of particular note - Pulau Tekong and the Western Catchment Area.

**Pulau Tekong** is a large island lying between the north-eastern shore of Singapore Island and the south-eastern corner of Peninsular Malaysia. The public is not allowed to land on any part of the island. Habitats include secondary forest, freshwater swamp forest, scrubland, plantations and mangrove. In recent years, researchers have recorded a number of significant finds. These include the East Asian Ornate Chorus Frog, Brown's Flap-legged Gecko, Kuhl's Gliding Gecko and Malayan Porcupine. A fair population of Leopard Cat, Sunda Slow Loris and Sunda Pangolin also exists there. In 1990, three Asian Elephants landed on Pulau Tekong after having swum across the Johor Straits, but they were promptly caught and returned to Malaysia.

Sunda Slow Loris

Leopard Cat

The **Western Catchment Area** comprises the general area of Singapore Island west of Jalan Bahar and Lim Chu Kang Road, and bordered in the south by the Ayer Rajah Expressway (AYE) and Pan Island Expressway (PIE). Habitats include grassland, secondary forest, freshwater swamp forest, scrubland, farmland, parkland and mangrove. Part of the area is occupied by the campus of the Nanyang Technological University, cemeteries and a number of farms. However most of the area is a restricted military training ground of the Singapore Armed Forces.

In recent years, Singapore's Ministry of Defence has been actively supporting wildlife surveys and research on Pulau Tekong and in the Western Catchment Area.

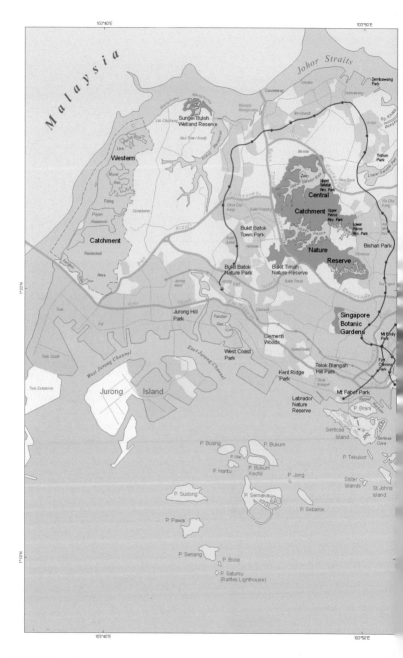

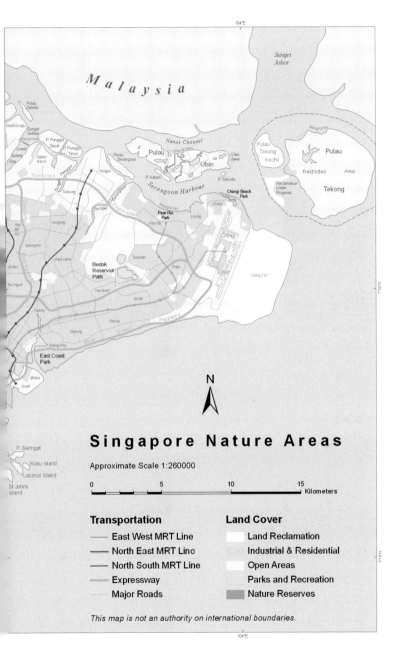

# Singapore Nature Areas

Approximate Scale 1:260000

0          5          10          15
Kilometers

## Transportation

— East West MRT Line
— North East MRT Line
— North South MRT Line
— Expressway
— Major Roads

## Land Cover

Land Reclamation
Industrial & Residential
Open Areas
Parks and Recreation
Nature Reserves

*This map is not an authority on international boundaries.*

# REGULATIONS AND SUGGESTIONS

Please respect the environment and the right of others to quietly enjoy nature, and observe the following do's and don'ts while exploring Singapore's nature areas.

## DO

- Adhere to regulations set by the National Parks Board when visiting nature reserves or public parks.

- Keep to marked or clearly established routes.

- Be careful where you put your feet to avoid crushing plants or wildlife.

- Walk quietly - you'll see more wildlife this way.

- Dress in earthy colours such as green and brown - you're less likely to disturb wildlife.

- Leave the trail cleaner than you found it. Carry out all litter.

- Report poachers to the relevant authorities - National Parks Board, Agri-veterinary Authority of Singapore (AVA) and Singapore Police Force.

- Report interesting sightings to the Vertebrate Study Group.

- Take and share photos of wildlife.

## DON'T

- Take a group of more than 40 people into the nature reserves without permission from the National Parks Board.

- Enter restricted areas.

- Damage or remove flowers and plants - leave them for others to enjoy.

- Touch or disturb wildlife.

- Feed wildlife, especially monkeys.

- Take dogs and other pets into the nature reserves.

- Release unwanted pets or other animals into the wild - most will soon die, often of starvation or disease.

# SPECIES IDENTIFICATION GUIDE

**Layout of text on species description**

ENGLISH VERNACULAR NAME

Scientific name: genus and species (scientific name used previously in other publications)

Order: Family. Maximum known size (see Measurements). Short list of diagnostic features. Habitat. Notes on ecology and biology. Taxonomic remarks (if any). Distribution and status in Singapore. World distribution.

**A note on scientific names**

The science of animal classification is an ongoing process. The limits that define each and every level of animal group (such as species, genus, family and order) change with the findings and opinions of researchers who work on the revisions. Many of the names in this book differ vastly from those in other publications as we try to provide the latest nomenclature. Names used previously in other publications are placed in brackets so that the reader is able to link the same animal species from different publications.

'*formerly as*' indicates that the name has since become a synonym of the present name. It may be a change in the genus, or it may be a completely different name. For example, the frogs *Fejervarya limnocharis* and *Hylarana erythraea* are known in earlier publications as *Rana limnocharis* and *Rana erythraea* respectively. The Forest Walking Catfish, *Clarias leiacanthus*, is known in previous publications as *Clarias teijsmanni*. Both names refer to the same fish, but *Clarias leiacanthus* is used here as it has precedence over the other.

'*formerly confused with*' indicates that the latter name is still in use, but since restricted to populations elsewhere. For instance, the Lesser Mousedeer from Southeast Asia was previously known as *Tragulus javanicus*. The latest research shows that *Tragulus javanicus* should be divided into a few distinct groups (populations), which are to be recognised as species. Since the name *Tragulus javanicus* was the original name given to the Javanese population, it is applied only to that group. The population in Singapore and southern peninsular Malaysia, however, needs a different name, and *Tragulus kanchil*, which was previously considered a synonym of *Tragulus javanicus*, was resurrected for this population.

**Measurements**

CL – carapace length (for turtles).

FA – forearm length (for bats).

HB – head and body length measured from tip of nose to anus (for mammals).

SL – standard length measured from tip of upper jaw to base of tail fin (for fishes).

SV – snout-vent length measured from tip of snout to cloaca (for frogs and some lizards).

TL – total length measured from tip of snout to tip of tail.

T – tail length measured from anus or cloaca to tip of tail.

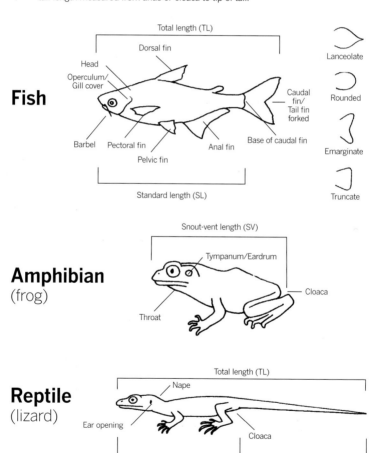

**Fish**

**Amphibian**
(frog)

**Reptile**
(lizard)

## Reptile
(snake)

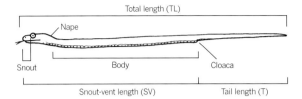

## Reptile
(turtle)

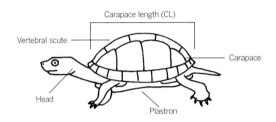

## Mammal
(rat)

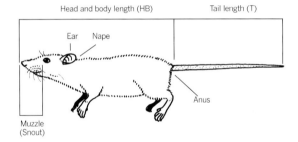

## Mammal
(bat)

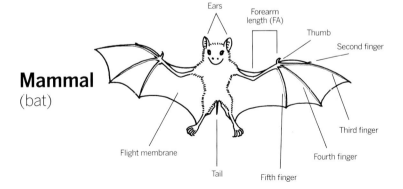

**Spanner Barbs
(*Systomus lateristriga*)**
Nick Baker

# FRESHWATER FISHES

The first vertebrates, primitive jawless fishes, evolved in the Cambrian period around 500 million years ago. These were superseded by hinged-jaw fishes during the Silurian period, some 430 million years ago. During the Devonian period, around 400 million years ago, bony fishes and cartilaginous fishes were both in existence; the fossil record indicates an evolutionary explosion of fish species at that time. To this day, fishes remain hugely diverse in body form and mode of life and occupy an immense variety of aquatic ecological niches.

Fishes can be simply defined as aquatic vertebrates which possess gills throughout life, whose limbs are in the form of fins, and whose skin is usually, but not exclusively, covered with scales. Most breathe in water, but some, for example the walking catfishes, swamp eels, anabantoid fishes and snakeheads, require access to atmospheric air at regular intervals or they will drown. Most fishes lay eggs, but some, for example the Guppy (a widely introduced species in Singapore), bear live young.

This book features only fish species that complete their entire life cycle in freshwater. In Singapore, freshwater habitats include forest streams, swamp-forest pools, rural ditches, artificial ponds and large impounding reservoirs. Except for one introduced species, all the freshwater fishes found in Singapore are bony fishes (class Osteichthyes).

The order Cypriniformes contains some of the more familiar forms of freshwater fish. They are characterised by a lack of teeth on their jaws, and instead have a pair of gill arches modified into a bone, bearing a series of pharyngeal teeth. Barbs and rasboras, some of the most visible species in our forest streams, are **CYPRINID FISHES** (family **Cyprinidae**). Members of this group tend to have one soft dorsal fin, and some have short barbels around the mouth that function as sensory organs. The carp and goldfish are well-known members of this family.

The **LOACHES** comprise two families of small, usually elongated, bottom-dwelling forms with short barbels around the mouth. Their bodies appear to be naked, but are, in fact, covered with minute scales. Loaches of the family **Nemacheilidae** (formerly as Balitoridae) differ from members of the **Cobitidae** in not having a spine below the eye.

The **CATFISHES** form the order Siluriformes. They come in various shapes and sizes, but they usually have up to four pairs of barbels around their mouths, and they are scaleless. However, members of the family Loricariidae, which includes the sucker-mouthed catfishes introduced from South America, have a series of hard plates covering their bodies. The walking catfishes (family **Clariidae**) have long sinuous bodies, long-based dorsal and anal fins, flattish heads and round to squarish tail fins. They breathe air and are adapted to survive in oxygen-poor waters. Their common name refers to the ability of some species to leave the water and "walk" with their pectoral fin spines over land to other bodies of water. The family **Siluridae** consists of laterally compressed fishes with a small dorsal fin, and a long-based anal fin. They tend to hide in submerged leaf litter during the day, but emerge at night and swim about in mid-water with undulating motions of the anal fin. Hasselt's Leaf Catfish is an example.

Not described in this book are three families of catfish that are native to Singapore's forest streams. The small, bottom-dwelling, rough-skinned catfishes belong to the family Akysidae. The forms with a pair of broad and flat barbels and a wrinkled area on the underside between the pectoral fins are in the family Sisoridae. The family Bagridae comprises larger, fork-tailed and smooth-skinned catfishes with a prominent adipose fin.

The order Cyprinodon-tiformes con-sists gener-

ally of small, slender fishes with prominent scales and a small dorsal fin. Because they have teeth in their squarish jaws, they are known as **TOOTHCARPS**. In Singapore, the family **Aplocheilidae** is native and lays eggs. The surface-dwelling Whitespot is the sole local representative. The family **Poeciliidae** comprises a few species from Latin America that were deliberately intro-duced for mosquito control. These include the Guppy and the Mosquitofish. They are known as "live-bearing toothcarps" because the anal fin of adult males is modified into an organ called the gonopo-dium, which is used to impregnate females through internal fertilisation. The young hatch from eggs within their mother's body and are expelled as swimming fry.

Members of the order Beloniformes

have generally elongate bodies and long, slender jaws. Most are marine or estuarine, but two species are confined to freshwater in Singapore. They are **HALFBEAKS** of the family Hemiramphidae, so named because their lower jaw is considerably longer than their upper jaw. These fish dwell just under the surface of the water where they feed on fallen insects, particularly ants. The anal fin of adult males is also modified into an organ for internal fertilisation, and the young are also live-born.

The order Syn-branchiformes contains two representa-tive families

of elongated eel-like fishes in Singapore. The **SWAMP EELS** (family **Synbranchidae**)

are long and slender creatures whose gill opening is a slit across the throat. They do not have pectoral fins, and their dorsal and caudal fins are much reduced. Swamp eels breathe air, and will drown if deprived access to the water surface. They spend the daylight hours in submerged burrows, but emerge at night to hunt for small fish and invertebrates. Another group, the SPINY EELS (family Mastacembelidae) are identi-fied by their long, proboscis-like snout, presence of rayed fins, and a series of short spines along the back. Spiny eels tend to hide in the substrate or among submerged vegetation, and are thus seldom seen.

The order Perciformes contains a vast array of forms that are characterised largely by having dorsal fins with hard spiny and simple rays in the front portion, and soft branching rays towards the rear. In some groups, these two portions are split into two separate fins: the spiny dorsal and the soft dorsal. Representatives of the families Ambassidae, Gobiidae, Eleotri-dae, Nandidae, Cichlidae, Anabantidae, Osphronemidae and Channidae are found in Singapore's freshwaters.

The GOBIES (family Gobiidae) and **GUDGEONS**

(family **Eleotridae**) tend to have cylindrical bodies with separate spiny and soft dorsal fins, and wide mouths. Most are bottom-dwelling carnivores. The gobies are gener-ally, but not always, distinguished from the gudgeons in having their pelvic fins fused into a sucker-like structure. The pelvic fins of the gudgeons are always separated.

**LEAF-FISHES**
belong to the family
**Nandidae**. These
small, laterally com-
pressed, large-eyed
fish are cryptically

coloured to resemble fragments of leaf lit-ter, and their body movements mimic dead leaves. Their cavernous mouths suggest their predatory nature. Leaf-fishes either stay still at one spot to ambush small fish or shrimps, or drift with the current to pounce on unsuspecting victims.

The **CICHLIDS** (family **Cichlidae**) are a group of introduced fishes that are  native to India, the Middle East, Africa and Latin America. They are usually laterally compressed with a continuous dorsal fin. Although they are gregarious, the males tend to be aggressive towards each other, and each will mark out a territory on the substrate. At least seven species have established feral populations in Singapore. The Mozambique Tilapia was introduced in the 1940s for aquaculture. Other species appeared in the last two decades as ornamental fishes, and were released into the wild by pet owners who had lost interest.

The **ANABANTOID FISHES** are all air-breathers, and many species in this group  can survive in waters deficient in oxygen. Provided they remain moist, a few species can even live for some time out of water. The climbing perch (family **Anabantidae**) has a robust body with long-based dorsal and anal fins, and prominent spines on its gill covers. It is renowned for its ability to wriggle over land from one water body to another rather like the walking catfishes, except that it is aided by its flared-out spiny gill covers. The family **Osphronemidae** (presently including the families Belontiidae and Luciocephalidae) consists of goramies, fighting fishes and pikeheads. Most of them have thread-like pelvic fins which can be used as tactile organs. Many anabantoids practise parental care for their brood. Goramies build bubble-nests for their spawn, and the males of the Malayan Pikehead and Malayan Forest Betta keep both the eggs and fry in their mouths.

**SNAKEHEADS** (family **Channidae**) are air-breathing fishes with cylindrical  bodies, long-based dorsal and anal fins, large pectoral fins and massive heads. They are predatory but exhibit parental care of their young. While the Dwarf Snakehead is a mouth-brooder, the Toman guards its brood of fry so fiercely that it is known to attack any creature that approaches too closely, including humans.

There are no native freshwater cartilaginous fishes (class Chondrichthyes) in Singapore. Fishes from this group, which includes sharks and rays, differ fundamentally from bony fishes in that their skeletons are composed of cartilage, and their gill openings are a series of slits. However, the Motoro Ray (*Potamotrygon motoro*), a popular ornamental fish native to South America, has been released into the wild in Singapore, where it is known to be breeding in one freshwater location.

The reader will notice many references to introduced fish species in this guide. Though there may be an ecological role for the carefully planned introduction of alien fishes into, for example, large man-made water bodies such as reservoirs, the uncontrolled release of alien fishes by the general public should be strongly discouraged, as it can have a potentially negative impact on populations of native species, many of which are already under threat of local extinction by other ecological pressures.

FRESHWATER FISHES

## BARBEL-LESS CHEMPERAS or RED-EYED BARB
*Cyclocheilichthys apogon*

Cypriniformes: Cyprinidae. To 20 cm TL. Body rhomboid, laterally compressed, and silver with black spots arranged in a longitudinal line across each scale row. Fins red, black blotch at caudal base, no barbels around mouth. Inhabits shaded forest streams where it dwells in mid-water, and feeds on small aquatic invertebrates. In Singapore, restricted to the Central Catchment Nature Reserve. Distributed in mainland Southeast Asia, Sumatra and Borneo.

Kelvin Lim

## EINTHOVEN'S RASBORA
*Rasbora einthovenii*

Cypriniformes: Cyprinidae. To 8 cm TL. Slender-bodied, grey above, abdomen silvery; a black stripe from snout to base of tail fin, and extending to fork of tail fin. Dorsal fin hyaline with a white tip and a black transverse stripe. Gregarious, omnivorous; inhabits the upper and middle water levels in shallow, slow-flowing and shaded streams. In Singapore, occurs in the Central Nature Reserves, Western Catchment Area and Pulau Tekong. Distributed in the Malay Peninsula, Sumatra and Borneo.

Nick Baker

## TWO-SPOT RASBORA
*Rasbora elegans*

Cypriniformes: Cyprinidae. To 12 cm TL. Slender-bodied, grey above, abdomen silvery; a squarish black blotch on mid-body under dorsal fin, smaller black blotch on base of tail, and a black streak above anal fin. Tail fin with black outer edge. Gregarious, insectivorous; inhabits the upper and middle water levels in forest streams. In Singapore, occurs in the Central Nature Reserves. Distributed in the Malay Peninsula, Sumatra and Borneo.

Nick Baker

## SADDLE BARB
*Systomus banksi* (formerly confused with *Puntius binotatus*)

Cypriniformes: Cyprinidae. To about 10 cm TL. Body rhomboid, pale golden or greyish silver with a triangular blackish blotch under dorsal fin and a blackish spot on caudal peduncle. Fins dusky with reddish tinge. Juveniles silvery with a slender black bar under the dorsal fin and two or more black spots on hind part of body. Mouth with two pairs of barbels. Gregarious omnivore that frequents the middle and lower water levels in forest streams. In Singapore, occurs in the Central Nature Reserves and Western Catchment Area. Distributed in the Malay Peninsula, Sumatra and Borneo.

Nick Baker

## SPANNER BARB or T-BARB
*Systomus lateristriga* (formerly as *Puntius lateristriga*)

Cypriniformes: Cyprinidae. To 18 cm TL. Body slender, dorsum in front of dorsal fin distinctly convex. Sides of body silver with two broad black bars on anterior half and one broad black stripe on posterior half. Mouth with two pairs of short barbels. Gregarious omnivore that frequents the middle and lower water levels in forest streams. In Singapore, found in the Central Catchment Nature Reserve. Distributed in the Malay Peninsula, Sumatra, Borneo and Java.

Nick Baker

## HARLEQUIN RASBORA
*Trigonostigma heteromorpha* (formerly as *Rasbora heteromorpha*)

Cypriniformes: Cyprinidae. To about 5 cm TL. Body rhomboid with slender caudal peduncle, pinkish, abdomen silvery; a black triangular blotch on the side, and an oblique, narrow black bar behind the gill cover. Shaded forest streams with acidic water. This gregarious fish lives in small streams and frequents the upper and middle water levels, and is mainly insectivorous. In Singapore occurs in the Central Catchment Nature Reserve. Distributed in the Malay Peninsula and Sumatra.

Norman Lim

# GREY-BANDED SAND LOACH
## *Nemacheilus selangoricus*

Cypriniformes: Nemacheilidae. To about 9 cm TL. Body cylindrical in cross-section with 3 pairs of short barbels, 8 to 12 regular grey bars, and a black spot at the base of the dorsal fin. Tail fin forked. This bottom-dwelling fish frequents fast flowing forest streams with acidic water, and sand-gravel substrate. In Singapore, known only from a small part of the Central Catchment Nature Reserve. Distributed in the Malay Peninsula, Sumatra and Borneo.

Nick Baker

# SPOTTED EEL-LOACH
## *Pangio muraeniformis*

Nick Baker

Cypriniformes: Cobitidae. To about 8 cm TL. Very slender, eel like, yellowish-brown with black blotches, 3 pairs of short barbels, and 3 black bars on the head. Tail fin slightly emarginate. Inhabits shaded forest streams with acidic water. This bottom-dwelling omnivore lives hidden away among dense submerged vegetation and leaf litter. In Singapore, known from one part of the Central Catchment Nature Reserve. Occurs elsewhere in southern Peninsular Malaysia and the Riau islands of Indonesia.

## HASSELT'S LEAF CATFISH
*Silurichthys hasseltii*

Siluriformes: Siluridae. To over 14 cm TL. Very slender and scaleless with two pairs of barbels, one pair considerably longer than the other; long anal fin fused to elongated tail fin, and small dorsal fin with only four rays. Body yellowish-brown mottled with dark brown. Inhabits well-shaded forest streams and swamps with acidic waters. This carnivorous fish swims about actively in mid-water at night. In Singapore, recorded only from the Central Catchment Nature Reserve. Distributed in the Malay Peninsula, Java and Sumatra.

Norman Lim

## COMMON WALKING CATFISH
*Clarias batrachus*

Siluriformes: Clariidae. To 40 cm TL. Slender (but less so than the Slender Walking Catfish) and scaleless with four pairs of long barbels, long dorsal and anal fins separate from tail fin. Narrow gap between origin of dorsal fin and back margin of exposed bony plates on head. Head oval when viewed from above. Body dark greyish-brown with vertical rows of tiny whitish spots on the sides. Inhabits waterways in disturbed and exposed habitats, even slightly polluted, concretised drains. Nocturnal, bottom-dwelling and carnivorous. Recorded from scrub and suburban areas throughout Singapore Island and Pulau Tekong. Widely distributed in India and Southeast Asia.

Norman Lim

## FOREST WALKING CATFISH
*Clarias leiacanthus* (formerly as *Clarias teijsmanni*)

Siluriformes: Clariidae. To about 40 cm TL. Slender (but less slender than Clarias nieuhofii) and scaleless with four pairs of long barbels, long dorsal and anal fins separate from tail fin.

Wide gap between origin of dorsal fin and back margin of exposed bony plates on head. Head squarish when viewed from above. Body greyish-brown with vertical rows of yellowish spots on the sides. Inhabits well-shaded forest streams and swamps with acidic waters. Nocturnal, bottom-dwelling and carnivorous. Recorded from the Central Catchment Nature Reserve. Distributed in the Malay Peninsula, Java, Sumatra and Borneo.

## SLENDER WALKING CATFISH
*Clarias nieuhofii*

Siluriformes: Clariidae. To 50 cm TL. Very slender and scaleless with four pairs of long barbels, long dorsal and anal fins partially fused to tail fin. Wide gap between origin of dorsal fin and back margin of exposed bony plates on head. Head squarish when viewed from above. Body greyish-brown with vertical rows of yellowish spots on the sides. Inhabits well-shaded forest streams and swamps with acidic waters. Nocturnal, bottom-dwelling and carnivorous. Recorded from the Central Catchment Nature Reserve and Pulau Tekong. Distributed in the Malay Peninsula, Java, Sumatra and Borneo.

## MALAYAN PYGMY HALFBEAK
*Dermogenys collettei* (formerly confused with *Dermogenys pusilla*)

Beloniformes: Hemiramphidae. To about 6 cm TL. Body slender; lower jaw considerably longer than, and protruding beyond upper jaw. Dorsal fin with short base, its origin behind anal fin origin. Body grey, dorsal fin marked with red. Gregarious surface-dweller that feeds largely on small insects. Females give birth to live young. Occurs in small streams and ponds in both forest and exposed areas, in freshwater and brackish water. In Singapore, land-locked populations found in the Central Nature Reserves and Western Catchment Area. Distributed in the Malay Peninsula and Sumatra.

Nick Baker

## MALAYAN FOREST HALFBEAK
*Hemirhamphodon pogonognathus*

Beloniformes: Hemiramphidae. To 9 cm TL. Body slender; lower jaw considerably longer than, and protruding beyond upper jaw. Dorsal fin with long base, its origin in front of anal fin origin. Body greyish brown with a thin red streak behind gill cover. Lower jaw red on underside, its tip fleshy and curving downwards. Gregarious surface-dweller that feeds largely on ants and other small insects. Females give birth to live young. In Singapore, confined to shaded forest streams in the Central Catchment Nature Reserve. Distributed in the Malay Peninsula, Sumatra, Borneo and Java.

Nick Baker

# WHITESPOT
## *Aplocheilus panchax*

Cyprinodontiformes: Aplocheilidae. To 6 cm TL. Top of head flattened, mouth upturned. Body slender, yellowish; a distinct shiny white spot on top of head between the rear edge of the eyes. Dorsal fin small with a black blotch in the middle. From side view, a blackish line along lower jaw. Inhabits the upper water levels in fresh and brackish waters. Gregarious and omnivorous. In Singapore, land-locked populations occur in the Central Nature Reserves. Also in streams and ditches in scrubland. Distributed from India, through Indochina, to Malaysia, and western Indonesia.

Nick Baker

# GUPPY
## *Poecilia reticulata*

Cyprinodontiformes: Poeciliidae. Females to 5 cm TL, males about half the size. Top of head flattened, mouth upturned. Male smaller than females, with front anal fin rays modified into a gonopodium. Males with black spots on lower side of body, body and often fins marked with red and blue. Females olive grey with unmarked fins and light outlines on the scales. Inhabits the upper and middle levels in fresh and brackish waters. Gregarious and omnivorous. Females give birth to live young. Domesticated varieties developed and produced in large numbers on ornamental fish farms. Introduced species in Singapore. Feral populations in many inland waterways, including roadside drains, throughout Singapore. Native to the West Indies and northern South America from Venezuela to Guyana.

Nick Baker

**Male (left) and female (right)**

# ORIENTAL SWAMP EEL
*Monopterus albus*

Synbranchiformes: Synbranchidae. To 40 cm TL. Body very slender, snake-like, smooth and superficially naked; tail tapers to a point. Dorsal and tail fins reduced to a very low and narrow ridge, no pectoral fin. Mouth large, eyes minute. Gill slit across throat. Brown with yellowish underside, often speckled with black. Solitary and nocturnal, often hiding in submerged burrows or among root mats. Needs to breathe atmospheric air, thus often seen with head sticking out of burrow towards water surface. Predatory on small fish, insects and crustaceans. Frequents streams, ditches, swamps and ponds. Widespread in Singapore, occurring even in monsoon canals, and is able to tolerate brackish water. Widespread in East Asia, and Southeast Asia.

Lim Swee Cheng

Nick Baker

# SUNDA LEAF-FISH
## *Nandus nebulosus*

Perciformes: Nandidae. To 13.5 cm TL. Oval-shaped and laterally compressed. Body brown, heavily mottled with black. Hind part of dorsal fin, anal fin, pectoral fins and tail fin translucent. Mouth very wide, its corners reaching to beneath hind margin of eye. Inhabits slow-flowing, well-shaded forest streams. This fish is solitary and with its cryptic coloration, bears a strong resemblance to a dead leaf. With this camouflage, it is able to sneak up to small fishes and prawns upon which it preys. In Singapore, found in the Central Nature Reserves. Distributed in the Malay Peninsula, Sumatra and Borneo.

# MOZAMBIQUE TILAPIA
## *Oreochromis mossambicus*

Perciformes: Cichlidae. To 38 cm TL. Body slender, oval-shaped; mouth large and oblique. Grey to olive above with three or four blackish blotches on the sides. Sexually active males with thick bluish upper lip, black body, white underside of head, red edges on dorsal and tail fins. Juveniles silver with six to eight blackish bars. Gregarious and omnivorous, inhabiting the middle and lower water levels. The male excavates shallow depressions in substrate in which he displays to passing females. The female broods the eggs and newly hatched fry in her mouth. Introduced species in Singapore. Brackish-water populations established in estuaries all over Singapore. Land-locked freshwater populations found in ponds, reservoirs and canals. Native to East Africa, but introduced to many parts of the world for aquaculture.

**Male (left) and female**

## MARBLED GUDGEON or SOON HOCK
*Oxyeleotris marmorata*

Perciformes: Eleotridae. To over 60 cm TL. Body cylindrical in cross-section and slender, head depressed with rounded snout, small eyes and large oblique mouth. Two dorsal fins; pelvic fins separate, pectoral fins large and round, reddish and with two blackish blotches at the base. Body pale greyish brown with three irregular dark brown bars on the hind part, and marbled blotches on the

front part. Nocturnal, solitary and carnivorous. It tends to lie motionless on the substrate to ambush small fish and shrimps. An important and esteemed food fish in Southeast Asia. In Singapore, found in the Central Catchment Nature Reserve, Lower Seletar Reservoir, and reservoirs in the Western Catchment Area. Distributed in Indochina, the Malay Peninsula, Sumatra, Borneo and the Philippines.

A N A B A N T O I D   F I S H E S

## ASIAN CLIMBING PERCH
*Anabas testudineus*

Perciformes: Anabantidae. To 23 cm TL. Body somewhat rectangular, head rounded. Edge of gill cover (operculum) serrated and with a black spot. Dorsal fin long-based, anterior two-thirds with spiny rays. Tail fin truncate. Body uniform olive-grey, sometimes with indistinct blackish bars. Occurs singly or in groups and keeps mainly to the lower water levels.

Omnivorous, it also eats small fish and insects. Breathes air and able to survive out of water if kept damp. In Singapore, found in streams and ponds in forest or rural areas. Widespread in India, East Asia, Indochina, Malaysia, Indonesia and the Philippines.

## MALAYAN PIKEHEAD
*Luciocephalus pulcher*

Perciformes: Osphronemidae. To 18 cm TL. Body elongated and cylindrical with a pointed snout, a deeply notched anal fin, and a broad brown stripe on its sides. This stripe is not very distinct when the fish is viewed from above, and it has blackish margins which are sometimes broken into spots. Topside brown, underside white with a thin black stripe along lower side of body. The mouth is telescopic and can be extended outwards to catch fish. This surface-dwelling fish inhabits shaded, slow flowing forest streams with acidic water. Ambush predator of small fish and shrimps. The male broods his eggs in his mouth. In Singapore, restricted to the Central Catchment Nature Reserve. Elsewhere, found in Peninsular Malaysia, Sumatra and Borneo.

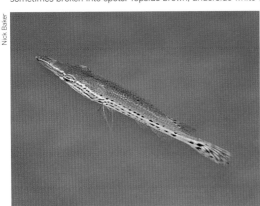

Nick Baker

## CROAKING GORAMY
*Trichopsis vittata*

Perciformes: Osphronemidae. To 6 cm TL. Body slender, laterally compressed; snout pointed. Tail fin lanceolate, anal fin broad-based with pointed tip at rear end. Body greyish brown with about four blackish stripes from head to base of tail fin; dorsal, anal and tail fins with reddish markings; eye with distinct blue ring. Frequents the upper water levels singly or in groups, and is omnivorous. The English name is derived from the fish's ability to produce a soft croaking sound during breeding activities. In Singapore, occurs in streams and ponds with dense vegetation in scrub and rural areas. Distributed in Indochina, the Malay Peninsula, Sumatra, Borneo and Java.

Nick Baker

# MALAYAN FOREST BETTA
## *Betta pugnax*

Perciformes: Osphronemidae. To 10 cm TL. Body slender, laterally compressed but head relatively robust. Tail fin round or lanceolate, anal fin broad-based with pointed tip at rear end. Depending on the fish's "mood", body brown with a greenish-blue spot on most scales, or brown with two blackish stripes from head to tail base. Throat of adults with iridescent green scales. Usually frequents shallow (under 30 cm depth) water, in groups, and among aquatic vegetation or leaf litter, in shaded forest streams. Omnivorous and appears to feed largely on insects. The male broods his eggs in his mouth. In Singapore, occurs in the Central Nature Reserves and the Western Catchment Area. Distributed in the Malay Peninsula and Sumatra.

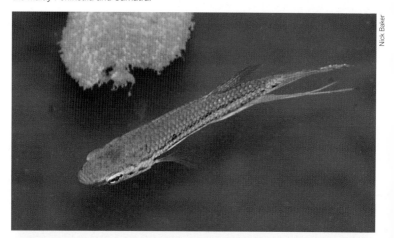

Nick Baker

Nick Baker

**Malayan Forest Betta with stripes (top) and without stripe.**

## THREE-SPOT GORAMY or SEPAT
*Trichogaster trichopterus*

Perciformes: Osphronemidae. To 15 cm TL. Body oval, laterally compressed, silvery-grey with a black spot at mid-body and another black spot on the base of tail fin. Tail fin emarginate, anal fin broad-based with orange spots, pelvic fins threadlike and used as tactile organs.

Frequents the upper water levels usually in groups, and is omnivorous. An airbreather, members of an entire group usually surface all at once to gulp air. In Singapore, occurs in streams and ponds with dense vegetation in scrub and rural areas. Distributed in Indochina, the Malay Peninsula, Sumatra, Borneo and Java.

Nick Baker

S N A K E H E A D S

## ARUAN or COMMON SNAKEHEAD
*Channa striata*

Perciformes: Channidae. To 90 cm TL (usually around 30 cm). Body slender, head relatively narrow. Body greyish brown above with irregular blackish bars. Underside white, distinct line of demarcation from dorsal colouration along side of body. In young specimens, a black spot present on rear end of dorsal fin. Predatory on fish, frogs and insects. Occurs alone or in pairs. Frequents sluggish streams and ponds in forest, scrub and rural areas. Also in reservoirs and concretised waterways. In Singapore, widespread and common. Distributed in India, Indochina, the Malay Peninsula, Sumatra, Borneo and Java.

Nick Baker

## DWARF SNAKEHEAD
*Channa gachua*

Perciformes: Channidae. 18 cm TL. Body slender, head broad and flattened. Body pale brown; dorsal, caudal and anal fins green to bluish with bright red or orange margins; pectoral fins with black bars. Inhabits shaded and shallow small streams and pools in swamp-forest. This nocturnal predator feeds on small fish, insects and crustaceans. The male broods eggs and fry in his mouth. In Singapore, known only from a small part of the Central Catchment Nature Reserve. Widespread in East and Southeast Asia, but there appears to be a complex of several species. Reported as extinct in Singapore in 1966, but rediscovered in 1989.

Kelvin Lim

## FOREST SNAKEHEAD or BUJUK
*Channa lucius*

Perciformes: Channidae. To 40 cm TL. Body slender, head tapering in side view. Brown on topside and fins, underside whitish. Oblique black stripe behind eye, round black blotch on upper gill cover, a series of black blotches along the sides, narrow black bars on underside. Fins with pearly spots. Juveniles of about 5 cm pale yellow with two black stripes from head to tail fin. Carnivorous, occurs alone or in pairs in shaded forest streams with acidic water. In Singapore, restricted to the Central Catchment Nature Reserve. Distributed in Indochina, the Malay Peninsula, Sumatra, Borneo and Java.

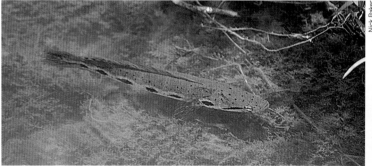

Nick Baker

## BLACK SNAKEHEAD
*Channa melasoma*

Perciformes: Channidae. To 28 cm TL. Body slender, head broad and relatively flat. Body grey to almost black; edges of caudal, anal and dorsal fins with very distinctive whitish margin; often a black spot at the posterior part of the dorsal fin. Fingerlings have black and orange stripes, and a white spot on top of the head. Frequents shaded forest streams with sluggish, acidic waters and submerged roots or leaf litter substrates. Apparently largely nocturnal and feeds on small animals. In Singapore, known only from the Central Nature Reserves. The species occurs in Peninsular Malaysia and Borneo. First reported from Singapore in 1990.

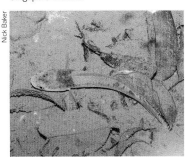

**Black Snakehead subadult (left) and adult**

## TOMAN or GIANT SNAKEHEAD
*Channa micropeltes*

Perciformes: Channidae. To 1 m TL. Body slender; adult with series of grey squarish blotches along the back; side with a broad black stripe from eye to tail fin, within this a row of white spots; underside white. Juveniles under 30 cm with two black stripes from snout to across tail fin, brown above and white on the underside, and red to yellow on the sides in between the two stripes. Diurnal predator of small fish and frogs, pelagic in habits and occurs usually in small groups. The young are highly gregarious. In Singapore, feral populations widespread in reservoirs and ponds. Native to large river systems in Southeast Asia.

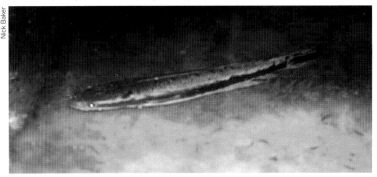

**Four-lined Tree Frogs (*Polypedates leucomystax*) spawning.**
Celine Low

# AMPHIBIANS

Amphibians are believed to have evolved directly from fish which first ventured onto dry land in the Devonian period, around 400 million years ago. They reach their highest diversity in the humid tropics, and globally there are reckoned to be around 6,000 species in existence.

Amphibians lack scales, which protect most fishes and reptiles, and fur, which insulates most mammals. Their skin is permeable to oxygen, both in and out of water, but when out of water they must remain reasonably moist to prevent dehydration. Like reptiles, amphibians are ectothermic or "cold-blooded".

Most amphibians lay eggs in water, and the young have to undergo a series of morphological changes as tadpoles before they metamorphose into adults with well-developed limbs. While almost all adult amphibians breathe air and are carnivorous, tadpoles breathe underwater and often feed on algae, vegetation and organic detritus.

Amphibians are freshwater animals that are generally intolerant of salt water. The Crab-eating Frog and its tadpoles, however, are often found in mangrove, and tadpoles of the Asian Frog are also sometimes found in brackish water.

The majority of amphibians in Singapore belong to the order Anura, which comprises the frogs and toads. Anurans have large heads joined directly to compact torsos. Their hind legs, distinctly longer than the fore limbs, are often extremely muscular which allows them to leap considerable distances relative to their body size. For example, the tiny chorus frogs, that measure around 2 cm from snout to vent, can easily cover a metre or more in a single jump, that is, over 50 times their body length.

In the humid tropics, frogs and toads may spend much time away from water without dehydrating, but in most cases must return to water to breed. After a heavy downpour, especially during the November to March rainy season, Singapore's freshwater ponds, forest streams and waterlogged grasslands play host to frogs eager to breed; the urgent calls of males trying to attract a mate may be heard from a considerable distance. Each species has a distinctive call, which enables members of the same species to identify and locate each other.

After spawning the resulting eggs float in the water in jellied masses or, in the case of the Asian Toad, in long gelatinous strings. Tadpoles emerge after some days, and hundreds may originate from a single pairing. Usually only one or two tadpoles survive to adulthood, the rest often being consumed by predators such as fishes or dragonfly larvae. To avoid being eaten some anuran tadpoles have evolved poison glands which makes them distasteful to predators. Other frogs have taken to breeding in such unlikely places as shallow roadside puddles, tree holes or, in the case of the Black-spotted Sticky Frog, the cups of pitcher plants. The common Four-lined Tree Frog builds foam nests which adhere to vegetation at the margins of small bodies of freshwater. The tadpoles initially develop inside the foam, but are washed into the water below during rain, there to complete their metamorphosis.

**TOADS** (family **Bufonidae**) can often be identified by their generally warty and drier skin, and by the presence 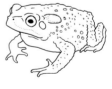 of a raised gland behind the eye. All other anurans, which tend to have smoother skin, are referred to as "frogs".

**FROGS** in Singapore fall into five families: The family **Megophryidae** (formerly as Pelobatidae) includes terrestrial frogs with relatively short and slender hind legs that only allow them to make short leaps. Rather than try to evade a potential threat, they prefer to conceal themselves among the substrate. With its brown, mottled skin, sharply pointed snout and angular appearance, the Malayan Horned Frog is a master of disguise. Even when calling loudly, this species is extremely difficult to locate in dry leaf litter.

Members of the family **Microhylidae** are called "narrow-mouthed frogs", for their heads and mouths tend to be relatively small. Representatives in Singapore have a tendency to burrow into the soil or hide in leaf-litter, and seem to feed largely on ants and termites. The Dark-sided Chorus Frog appears to be the most common, its presence being advertised by its repeated high-pitched rattling call.

The family **Ranidae** comprises frogs with slender bodies, pointed snouts, long muscular hind limbs and prominent tympanum (external ear drums). Some species have the tips of their digits expanded into discs.

The family **Dicroglossidae** (formerly as Ranidae) comprises large-headed robust frogs with muscular hind  limbs. They are semi-aquatic to aquatic in habits, and include some of the largest frogs in Southeast Asia. The Malayan Giant Frog is Singapore's largest frog, potentially reaching a maximum size of 26 cm, measured from snout to vent. Some dicroglossid species have a pair of prominent fangs on their jaws.

Members of the family **Rhacophoridae** are called "tree frogs" or "bush frogs". Most are arboreal, and the tips of their digits are expanded into sticky disks to facilitate climbing among vegetation. Unlike other Singapore anurans, some species have webbing between their fingers. Some rhacophorids have extensive webbing on both hands and feet which enables them to glide through the air. Such "flying frogs" are not present in Singapore, but can be found in neighbouring countries, including Malaysia and Indonesia.

The poorly known CAECILIANS (order Gymnophiona) are unlike frogs or toads in appearance.  With their long, rubbery, limbless body, short tail and tiny eyes, they may easily be mistaken for a worm or eel. Southeast Asian species reach up to 40 cm in length. Caecilians spend a large part of their lives underground feeding on soil-dwelling invertebrates, and are thus seldom seen. Two species are recorded from Singapore, and one of them, *Ichthyophis singaporensis*, known only from a single specimen collected in the late 1800s, may be endemic to our island.

There are no crawling amphibians, such as salamanders or newts (order Urodela), in Singapore.

Around one-third of Singapore's frog and toad species are able to thrive in man-made habitats such as city parks and gardens. The remaining species, mainly forest specialists, continue to survive in severely reduced habitat. Some, like the Copper-cheeked Frog, remain common throughout the Central Nature Reserves. Others, such as the Thorny Bush Frog, appear to be confined to small areas of the Bukit Timah Nature Reserve.

Amphibians should not be handled unless absolutely necessary; some exude a sticky mucus which may irritate sensitive skin, or may cause inflammation if inadvertently rubbed into the eye. Conversely, harmful toxins on human skin, such as from insect repellant or sunblock, may be absorbed through the skin of an amphibian and cause it harm.

Globally, amphibians are under considerable pressure from climate change, habitat destruction, pollution and fungal infestations. Tragically, many colourful and unique species are likely to become extinct in the coming decades.

**Banded Bull Frogs
(*Kaloula pulchra*)
spawning.**
Kelvin Lim

**Malesian Frog
(*Limnonectes malesianus*)
apparently guarding its
nest of eggs.**
Kelvin Lim

## ASIAN TOAD
*Duttaphrynus melanostictus* (formerly as *Bufo melanostictus*)

Anura: Bufonidae. To about 11 cm SV. Body robust, hind limbs relatively short and slender with highly reduced webbing. Skin distinctly warty, body and limbs grey to yellowish brown above. Raised, long, oval-shaped gland along side of head. Two black low ridges on top of head. Tadpoles small (about 1 cm) and blackish. This solitary, nocturnal and terrestrial insectivore is commensal with humans. The call is like a rapid, high-pitched series of "kwa-kwa-kwa" and is usually heard before and after heavy rain both in the day and in the evening. It is usually found in built-up areas but also occurs inside forest. In Singapore, common almost everywhere, even in coastal areas and on islands where its tadpoles are known to live in brackish water. Widely distributed in the Indian subcontinent and Southeast Asia.

Chan Kwok Wai

## FOUR-RIDGED TOAD
*Ingerophrynus quadriporcatus* (formerly as *Bufo quadriporcatus*)

Anura: Bufonidae. To about 6 cm SV. Body robust, hind limbs relatively short and slender, with highly reduced webbing. Skin distinctly warty, body and limbs usually bright orange-brown (sometimes dark brown) above. Raised gland along side of head very slender. Four low ridges on top of the head. Inhabits swampy areas in forest and at forest edges. Insectivorous, terrestrial and probably nocturnal, but will call ("kree-kroo, kree-kroo") from under leaf-litter during the day, especially before rain. In Singapore, known from the Central Nature Reserves, the Western Catchment Area, and Pulau Tekong. Occurs in the Malay Peninsula, Sumatra and Borneo.

Nick Baker

Chan Kwok Wai

## MALAYAN HORNED FROG
*Megophrys nasuta*

Anura: Megophryidae. To 16 cm SV. Body robust, snout sharply pointed, hind limbs relatively short and slender. Skin largely smooth with a few warts on the sides, and four longitudinal ridges along the back. A pair of horn-like skin flaps above the eyes. Mottled grey to brown over the back and on the topside of the limbs. This terrestrial, nocturnal, solitary carnivore lives as an ambush predator, well-camouflaged among dead leaves on

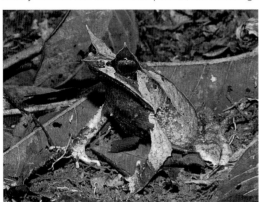

the floor of mature forests. Its call resembles a metallic honk and can be heard at dusk and just before rain. The tadpoles are mottled dark brown and have an upward-directing mouth with broad fleshy lips, and inhabit shallow forest streams with clear running water. In Singapore, confined to the Central Nature Reserves. Distributed in the Malay Peninsula, Borneo and Sumatra.

## BLACK-EYED LITTER FROG
*Leptobrachium nigrops*

Anura: Megophryidae. To 5 cm SV. Head large, limbs short and slender. Grey or brown with black irregular blotches on the back and sides. Underside white with dense blackish specks. Eyes black. Tadpoles almost entirely black and large (about 4 cm), and live in forest streams. This nocturnal, solitary insectivore lives among leaf litter on the forest floor. Its call, resembling a rattling gurgle, can be heard at dusk. In Singapore, confined to the Central Nature Reserves. Distributed in the Malay Peninsula and Borneo.

# CRAB-EATING FROG or MANGROVE FROG
*Fejervarya cancrivora* (formerly as *Rana cancrivora*)

Anura: Dicroglossidae. To over 8 cm SV. Body robust, hind legs long and muscular, hind feet extensively webbed, head large and broad. Skin on back with short low ridges. Back greyish brown with irregular blackish blotches and an oblique yellowish stripe on the sides. Throat of adult males white with a dark grey patch at the corners of the jaw. The brown-mottled tadpoles are quite large (about 3 cm) and live at the bottom of shallow pools and ditches. The adult is a nocturnal, semi-aquatic carnivore. The call resembles a drawn-out high-pitched rattling bray and is often heard in the evening. This species is partially commensal with humans and occurs in built-up areas. It tolerates brackish water, and is frequently found in mangroves. Also occurs in scrubland, parkland, and even in disturbed forest. In Singapore, common along the coast and on surrounding islands. Distributed in Indochina and the Philippines, the Malay Peninsula, Borneo, Sumatra and Java.

Chan Kwok Wai

# FIELD FROG or GRASS FROG
*Fejervarya limnocharis* (formerly as *Rana limnocharis*)

Anura: Dicroglossidae. To 6 cm SV. Hind legs long and muscular, hind feet half-webbed, head longer than broad. Skin on back with short, low ridges. Back grey or brown with irregular blackish blotches. Throat of adult males with a blackish band between the corners of the jaw. The brown-mottled tadpoles are about 2.5 cm and live at the bottom of shallow puddles and ditches. The adult is a nocturnal, terrestrial insectivore. Its call is similar to that of the Asian Toad, but more abrupt, starting out slow, but becoming faster towards the end, and is usually heard in the evening before and after heavy rain. This species is commensal with humans and is more common in built-up and disturbed habitats, especially in fields and scrubland, and also in forest clearings. In Singapore, common in suburban and rural areas. Distributed in Sri Lanka, India, Japan, Taiwan, southern China, the Philippines, Indochina, the Malay Peninsula, Borneo, Sumatra and Java.

Chan Kwok Wai

# MALAYAN GIANT FROG
*Limnonectes blythii* (formerly as *Rana blythii*, and confused with *Rana macrodon*)

Anura: Dicroglossidae. To 26 cm SV. Body robust, hind legs long and muscular, hind feet extensively webbed, head large and slightly longer than wide. Skin on back relatively smooth in large adults, warty in juveniles. Back brown or grey, with or without a broad yellowish mid-dorsal stripe. Throat whitish. In Singapore, there may be more than one species presently known under this name. Males grow larger than females. The call sounds like a low-pitched moan. This nocturnal, semi-aquatic carnivore occurs along streams in forest and scrubland. In Singapore, it occurs in the Central Nature Reserves, Western Catchment Area, the Botanic Gardens and Sungei Buloh Wetland Reserve. Distributed in Thailand, Peninsular Malaysia and Sumatra.

Nick Baker

Nick Baker

**Above: Large adult**
**Left: Adult with prominent vertebral stripe**
**Below: Mottled juvenile**

Nick Baker

## MALESIAN FROG
*Limnonectes malesianus* (formerly as *Rana malesiana*, and confused with *Rana macrodon*)

Anura: Dicroglossidae. To 15 cm SV. Body robust, hind legs long and muscular, hind feet extensively webbed, head large and broad. Skin on back smooth, back reddish brown with a very thin white stripe down the middle and several small blackish blotches on the sides.

Half of ear drum blackish. Throat mottled dark grey with a white dividing line down the middle. Males grow larger than females. This nocturnal, semi-aquatic carnivore occurs in mature swampy forest. In Singapore, occurs mainly in the Central Nature Reserves and also in the Western Catchment Area. Distributed in the Malay Peninsula, Borneo, Sumatra and Java.

Norman Lim

## MASKED SWAMP FROG
*Limnonectes paramacrodon* (formerly as *Rana paramacrodon*)

Anura: Dicroglossidae. To 7 cm SV. Hind legs long and slender, tips of fingers and toes not flattened into disks. Skin rough and uniformly brown over back. A black mask covers most of the tympanum (but this mask is not distinct on individuals from Pulau Tekong), abdomen yellow. Inhabits freshwater swamp forest. Nocturnal, insectivorous and semi-aquatic, usually seen on banks of small streams. Does not seem to call. Larval stages not known. In Singapore, known from the Central Catchment Nature Reserve and Pulau Tekong. Distributed in the Malay Peninsula, Sumatra and Borneo.

Nick Baker

## RHINOCEROS FROG
*Limnonectes plicatellus* (formerly as *Rana plicatella*)

Norman Lim

Anura: Dicroglossidae. To about 4 cm SV. Body short and squat, head broad and massive, hind legs long and relatively muscular. Back with a series of low longitudinal ridges, orange or brown with irregular grey blotches. Adult males have a backward-pointing bony protrusion on top of the head. Its call is a series of deep, long-drawn, crescendo croaks, and is usually heard in the evening. Nocturnal, semi-aquatic insectivore that frequents shallow streams in mature forest. In Singapore, confined to the Central Nature Reserves. This species appears to be endemic to the Malay Peninsula.

## YELLOW-BELLIED PUDDLE FROG
*Occidozyga sumatrana* (formerly confused with *Occidozyga laevis*)

Anura: Dicroglossidae. To about 4 cm SV. Body squat with relatively small head. Hind legs long and muscular with large fully webbed feet. Brown or yellow above, some individuals have a white or orange stripe down the middle of the back. Its call is a rubbery-sounding "ek-ek-ek", and is usually heard in the evening. Nocturnal, insectivorous and largely aquatic in habits. It occurs

Chan Kwok Wai

along forest streams and puddles, and is often seen immersed in shallow water except for the top of the head and eyes which protrude above the surface. In Singapore, it occurs in swampy areas of the Central Nature Reserves, the Western Catchment Area and Pulau Tekong. Distributed in the Malay Peninsula, Borneo, Sumatra and Java.

## CINNAMON BUSH FROG or SPOTTED TREE FROG
*Nyctixalus pictus*

Anura: Rhacophoridae. To 3.5 cm SV. Limbs long and slender, feet with expanded flattened tips to digits. Brown or reddish brown with irregular white or yellowish spots on topside of body and limbs. This nocturnal insectivore is arboreal, usually found on low shrubs. It breeds in tree holes, and the tadpoles are blackish with eyes positioned on top of the head. The call of the males, a soft "poop" is usually heard in the evening. In Singapore, apparently confined to the Central Nature Reserves. Distributed in the Malay Peninsula, Sumatra, Borneo and Palawan.

Chan Kwok Wai

## FOUR-LINED TREE FROG or COMMON TREE FROG
*Polypedates leucomystax* (formerly as *Rhacophorus leucomystax*)

Anura: Rhacophoridae. To 7.5 cm SV. Skin relatively smooth, limbs long and slender, feet with expanded flattened tips to digits. Brown, grey or yellow on the back, with or without four thin blackish stripes. This nocturnal insectivore is arboreal, usually found on shrubs and long grass. The call, resembling a loud nasal quack, is usually heard in the evening. Females are considerably larger than males. The eggs are laid in a foam nest suspended over a water body where the tadpoles drop when the nest disintegrates during heavy rain. Tadpoles are large (about 3 cm), with a dark greyish-brown body and white abdomen, and a small but distinct white spot on top of the snout. Commensal with humans, adults are frequently encountered in buildings. In Singapore, common in suburban and rural habitats, but also occurs in disturbed forest. Distributed in southern China and Indochina, the Malay Peninsula, Borneo, Sumatra, Java and the Philippines.

**Frogs with stripes and without stripes**

Norman Lim

Nick Baker

# BLUE-SPOTTED BUSH FROG
*Rhacophorus cyanopunctatus* (formerly confused with *Rhacophorus bimaculatus*)

Anura: Rhacophoridae. To about 4 cm SV. Skin relatively smooth, limbs long and slender, feet with expanded flattened tips to digits. Brown or beige above with dark brown transverse blotches over back and top of head. Distinct white spot on upper lip under eye. Underside of thigh with small bluish spots. Tadpoles (to 2.5 cm) are slender, black,

with downward-facing mouth. Nocturnal and arboreal. Lives in vegetation along streams in mature forest, and feeds on small invertebrates. In Singapore, known from the Central Catchment Nature Reserve. Distributed in the Malay Peninsula, Sumatra and Borneo.

# THORNY BUSH FROG
*Theloderma horridum*

Anura: Rhacophoridae. To 4 cm SV. Skin distinctly warty, limbs long and slender, feet with expanded flattened tips to digits. Mottled grey and brown above with a broad cream chevron marking over the back. Nocturnal and arboreal. Has been observed on the trunks of large trees in mature forest. Due to its cryptic colouration, this frog blends in very well with tree bark, and is difficult to see. In Singapore, recorded only from Bukit Timah Nature Reserve. Distributed in the Malay Peninsula, Sumatra and Borneo. First reported in Singapore in 1996.

## GOLDEN-EARED ROUGH-SIDED FROG
*Pulchrana baramica* (formerly as *Rana baramica*)

Chan Kwok Wai

Anura: Ranidae. To 7 cm SV. Skin on back and sides warty, hind legs long and slender, tips of fingers and toes not flattened into disks. Topside greyish brown with dark brown blotches, ear drum brown with gold spot in the centre. Upper lip white with brown bands. This largely terrestrial, nocturnal insectivore inhabits swampy forest. Its call, a rapid "kwuck-kwuck-kwuck" is usually heard in the evening. In Singapore, it occurs in the Central Catchment Nature Reserve, the Western Catchment Area and Pulau Tekong. Distributed in the Malay Peninsula, Borneo, Sumatra and Java.

## MASKED ROUGH-SIDED FROG
*Pulchrana laterimaculata* (formerly confused with *Rana baramica*)

Nick Baker

Anura: Ranidae. To 4.5 cm SV. Skin on back and sides warty, hind legs long and slender, tips of fingers and toes not flattened into disks. Topside brown with blackish blotches, ear drum black. Upper lip entirely white. This largely terrestrial, nocturnal insectivore inhabits swampy forest where it often occurs together with the Golden-eared Rough-sided Frog. Its call, a loud and continuous high-pitched "yip-yip-yip" is usually heard in the evening. In Singapore, it occurs in the Central Nature Reserves and Pulau Tekong. Distributed in the Malay Peninsula and Borneo. Previously confused with the Golden-eared Rough-sided Frog.

# GREEN PADDY FROG or COMMON GREENBACK
## *Hylarana erythraea* (formerly as *Rana erythraea*)

Anura: Ranidae. To 7.5 cm SV. Skin on back smooth, hind legs long and slender, tips of fingers and toes not flattened into disks. Topside bright green, sometimes brown, with two brown-edged white stripes; upper lip white. Tadpoles are large (about 3 cm), marbled brown and green, and usually occur in still water in ponds and ditches. Adults are mainly

Nick Baker

nocturnal, insectivorous and amphibious, usually found at the water's edge or sitting on broad floating leaves like those of water-lilies. It is commensal with humans and occurs largely in freshwater bodies. Its call has been described as a "squeaky warble". In Singapore, common along the edge of freshwater lakes and ponds in suburban and rural areas. Widespread in Indochina, the Malay Peninsula, Borneo, Sumatra, Java, Sulawesi and the Philippines.

# COPPER-CHEEKED FROG or FOREST GREENBACK
## *Hydrophylax raniceps* (formerly confused with *Rana chalconota*)

Anura: Ranidae. To 7 cm SV. Skin on back relatively smooth, hind legs long and slender, tips of fingers and toes flattened into disks. Upper lip white, and a dark-brown mask over the side of head and ear drum. The entire back of the body and limbs are bright green, but at night, these areas may turn brown with darker markings. Tadpoles are yellow or orange with a blackish bar under the eyes, and a pair of white stripes (consisting of poison glands) on the belly. They are often found in forest streams with running water. The nocturnal and insectivorous adults are semi-arboreal, usually found on shrubs along water courses. The call

Chan Kwok Wai

resembles the sound of dripping water. There appears to be two forms (most likely separate species): one being larger and darker, the other is smaller and pale. Both forms often occur together. In Singapore, this species is found in the Central Nature Reserves, the Western Catchment Area and on Pulau Tekong. Distributed in the Malay Peninsula, Borneo and Sumatra.

## BANDED BULL FROG
*Kaloula pulchra*

Anura: Microhylidae. To 7.5 cm SV. Body rotund, head relatively small, hind limbs short and slender. Tips of fingers and toes expanded and with blunt tips. Back grey or brown with a pair of black-edged, broad pale yellow or orange stripes along the sides, and a pale yellow or orange band on top of the head between the eyes. This solitary and nocturnal insectivore (apparently feeds mainly on ants) is commensal with humans, inhabiting

built-up areas. The call, usually heard before and after heavy rain, resembles the mournful bellow of cattle. Although largely terrestrial, individuals have been found high up on tree trunks. In Singapore, believed to be an introduced species. It is common throughout the island from the coastal areas to the forest of the Central Nature Reserves, and also on offshore islands. Widely distributed from India and Sri Lanka, southern China and Indochina, through the Malay Peninsula, Borneo, Sumatra, Java and Sulawesi to the Philippines.

Chan Kwok Wai

## BLACK-SPOTTED STICKY FROG
*Kalophrynus pleurostigma*

Anura: Microhylidae. To over 5 cm SV. Body triangular when viewed from above, head relatively small, hind limbs short and slender with very reduced webbing. Snout pointed. Back pale brown or grey sharply demarcated from the dark brown on the sides. A black spot on the groin area just in front of the hind legs, usually hidden by the upper thigh when frog is

in crouching position. Tadpoles are grey above with white bellies, and are known to inhabit the terrestrial cups of a species of pitcher plant. Adults are solitary, nocturnal insectivores that live largely among the leaf litter on the forest floor. The call, a soft "pu-pu-pu" is usually heard in the evening. Apparently confined to the Central Nature Reserves. Distributed in the Malay Peninsula, Borneo, Sumatra, Java and the Philippines.

Norman Lim

## PAINTED CHORUS FROG
*Microhyla butleri*

Anura: Microhylidae. To 2.5 cm SV. Head relatively small, hind limbs relatively long and slender. Back and sides dark brown, a wavy yellowish stripe on the sides. An oblique yellowish streak behind the eye. Hind limbs with dark brown bands. Tadpoles (about 2 cm) have a large head and are transluscent, with reddish tail and blackish fins. They are found in still water in ponds and ditches, quietly hovering in midwater. This ground-dwelling, nocturnal insectivore is commensal with humans. It is found in gardens and scrubland and, in Singapore, is common in suburban and rural habitats as well as in disturbed forest. Distributed in southern China, Indochina and the Malay Peninsula.

Nick Baker

## EAST ASIAN ORNATE CHORUS FROG
*Microhyla fissipes*

Anura: Microhylidae. To about 2.5 cm SV. Head relatively small, hind limbs relatively long and slender. Back and sides dark olive brown, with a broad yellowish stripe along the sides (including two or three thin brownish stripes), and an oblique yellowish streak behind the eyes. This terrestrial, nocturnal insectivore breeds in muddy puddles. In Singapore, known only from young secondary forest on Pulau Tekong where it was first reported in 2005. It appears to be an introduced species in Singapore. Distributed in Japan, China, Indochina, the Malay Peninsula and Sumatra.

Chan Kwok Wai

## DARK-SIDED CHORUS FROG
*Microhyla heymonsi*

Anura: Microhylidae. To 2.5 cm SV. Head relatively small, hind limbs relatively long and slender. Back yellowish brown with a thin white stripe along the middle, a black stripe along the sides of the head and body, hind limbs with brownish bands, underside whitish. Tadpoles are small (about 1 cm) with a striking white band on top of the head between the eyes. They are surface dwellers and are usually found in still water in pools and ditches. This nocturnal and terrestrial insectivore is com-mensal with humans. Its call consists of a series of high-pitched "kriiiiiick" and is usu-ally heard in the evening. The caller, however, is difficult to find for it is usually concealed amongst grasses and leaf litter. In Singapore, common in suburban and rural areas, as well as in disturbed forest. Distributed in southern China and Taiwan, Indochina, the Malay Peninsula and Sumatra.

Nick Baker

## MANTHEY'S CHORUS FROG
*Microhyla mantheyi* (formerly confused with *Microhyla borneensis*)

Anura: Microhylidae. To about 2 cm SV. Head relatively small, hind limbs relatively long and slender. Back dark brown, paler towards the sides; sides blackish; top of the head between the eyes and snout yellowish brown; hind limbs with blackish bands. An oblique yellowish streak behind the eyes. Vent opening in the centre of a large black spot. Tadpoles (about 1.5 cm) have upturned lips that are directed towards the water surface to feed on floating organic par-ticles. Their tail tips are drawn into a thin fila-ment. This nocturnal and terrestrial insec-tivore inhabits forest. In Singapore it seems confined to the Central Nature Reserves where it was first reported in 1997 as Microhyla borneensis. Distributed in the Malay Peninsula.

Leong Tzi Ming

# TADPOLES

All of Singapore's frog and toad species have fully aquatic larval stages. Depending on the species, suitable water bodies might include permanent forest streams, temporary puddles, ornamental ponds, or even the cups of pitcher plants. Tadpoles are as varied in their colours, markings, morphology and sizes as are their respective adult forms. Some examples of tadpoles photographed in Singapore are shown here.

Asian Toad

Black-eyed Litter Frog

Green Paddy Frog

Masked Rough-sided Frog

Copper-cheeked Frog

Field Frog

Dark-sided Chorus Frog

Painted Chorus Frog

Four-lined Tree Frog

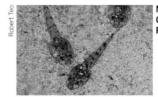
Malayan Giant Frog

**Paradise Gliding Snake**
**(*Chrysopelea paradisi*)**
Nick Baker

# REPTILES

The earliest reptiles evolved in the Carboniferous period, around 300 million years ago and, in the Jurassic and Cretaceous periods from 200 to 65 million years ago, gave rise to the dinosaurs which in turn gave rise to birds. Modern reptiles are a hugely diverse class of animals, which reach their greatest diversity in the tropics.

Most reptiles are covered with scales, never by hair or feathers. The scales may overlap each other, closely abut each other like mosaic, or be fused to form large rigid plates like those on the carapace of turtles.

Reptiles are ectothermic or 'cold-blooded'. This means they are unable to regulate their body temperature by cellular processes, instead they attempt to do so by making use of external sources of warmth. In most cases this is achieved by basking in direct sunlight until the body temperature is sufficiently elevated to allow the animal to become fully active. In the tropics, however, there is often sufficient warmth for many reptiles to be active at night.

Because body heat is not generated internally as it is, for example, by mammals and birds, reptiles require far less food. Some snake species may survive for many weeks without eating.

Reptiles are generally oviparous or egg-laying, but there are many species of snake which are ovo-viviparous, where eggs hatch inside the adult and live young are subsequently born. Clutch sizes can vary from just two eggs in many species of lizard to over 100 eggs in some species of turtle. Reproduction is generally sexual, but there are some lizard and snake species which are parthenogenetic. This means the females are able to produce eggs without being fertilised by a male. A local example of parthenogenesis is the tiny, burrowing Brahminy Blind Snake.

The diversity of Singapore's reptiles is relatively high, and many vulnerable forest-dependent species have survived habitat disturbance and habitat reduction.

New species records for Singapore are still being documented. Brown's Flap-legged Gecko, Five-banded Flying Dragon, Bigeye Green Whip Snake and Elegant Bronzeback were recorded for the first time after the year 2000. It is possible that more species are waiting to be discovered.

In Singapore, reptiles comprise four basic body forms all familiar to the lay-person. These are lizards, snakes, crocodiles and turtles.

**LIZARDS** (order Squamata, suborder Sauria) generally have an elongate  body, four legs and a long tail. Many of them have eyelids, and most have a small external ear-opening.

Local representatives of the dragon-lizards (family **Agamidae**) tend to have long-legs, short-heads, very long tails, and are covered in rough scales. Many of them have a row of spines down the back of their head, neck and torso. They are diurnal and live in trees and bushes, descending to the ground to lay their eggs or to move to another tree. The introduced Changeable Lizard occurs in most gardens and would have been seen by most people. Perhaps less familiar are the three local species of gliding lizard or 'flying dragon', which the observant may spot clinging to tree trunks, often well camouflaged. These small, slender lizards possess an extendable flap of skin (patagium) supported by extensions of their ribs, which allows them to quietly glide from tree to tree. Males have an extendable, brightly coloured throat flap or 'gular flag' which is displayed during territorial disputes or when trying to attract a mate.

Geckos (family **Gekkonidae**) are characterised by their relatively thin and delicate skin with tiny scales and large, lid-less eyes. They can be either nocturnal or diurnal in habits. When grasped by the tail, they are capable of readily shedding that appendage, however a new tail will eventually grow to replace the lost one. Some geckos have their fingers and toes expanded and lined beneath with a series of skin flaps with numerous microscopic hook-like hairs. These enable them to walk vertically on walls and even upside-down on the ceiling. Geckos are perhaps the most familiar of local reptiles. Rare is the house or apartment which does not have a resident gecko feeding on insects and laying its tiny, fragile eggs in some nook or cranny.

Members of the family Eublepharidae are also geckos, but differ in having eye-lids. One species is represented in Singapore, the Fox-faced Gecko (*Aeluroscalabotes felinus*). As there are no local field photographs of this rare and elusive creature, it is thus omitted from this book.

Skinks (family **Scincidae**) are generally long-bodied, short-legged lizards covered in smooth and large, shiny scales. Some species are ground-dwelling, such as the Common Sun Skink which abounds in our forest and gardens, while others are arboreal or semi-aquatic. There are even burrowing forms, which tend to either have very short legs, sometimes only two legs, or even no legs like a snake. These legless skinks have not been recorded in Singapore, however.

Monitors (family **Varanidae**) are large, ponderous lizards with a distinct forked tongue which is constantly flicked in and out of the mouth to 'taste' the air for the scent of food. They are largely carnivorous, feeding on insects and small vertebrates, but the larger species also scavenge for carcasses. The Malayan Water Monitor, sometimes seen along urban canals in Singapore, is one of the largest lizards in the world reaching up to 3 metres in total length, and only exceeded in bulk by the famed Komodo Dragon of Indonesia. Although largely terrestrial in habits, the Malayan Water Monitor usually lives along bodies of water, and is an excellent swimmer. It is also an able tree climber like its cousin, the Clouded Monitor.

**SNAKES** (order Squamata, suborder Serpentes) have a long, slender body,  lid-less eyes, no ear-openings, and no limbs (some lizards are legless, but they tend to have eyelids and ear-openings). Like monitor lizards, all snakes have a forked tongue which is used as an olfactory organ. All are carnivorous, and most swallow their prey whole.

The family **Typhlopidae** comprises burrowing snakes characterised by a blunt, rounded snout, tiny eyes, and a head that is indistinct from the body. They also have a very short, stumpy tail which, in some species, ends in a spine. The tiny Brahminy Blind Snake may well be common in gardens, but is rarely noticed on account of its diminutive size and burrowing habits and, no doubt, has frequently been mistaken for a worm. Upon closer scrutiny however, it can be seen to be covered in minute scales, have a tiny pair of eyes, and a small flickering tongue.

The family Cylindrophiidae comprises one species in Singapore: the Red-tailed Pipe Snake (*Cylindrophis ruffus*). It resembles a blind snake in appearance, but has a very distinct black-and-white chequered underside, and the tail is red beneath. It is live-bearing and seems to live in marshy areas where it is known to feed on frogs and other snakes.

The family **Pythonidae** comprises large, muscular, non-venomous snakes with heat-sensory pits on their lips. Some species have evolutionary remnants of limbs, visible externally as a pair of spurs, located near the vent (cloaca). Pythons are renowned for killing their prey by constriction, wrapping their body around the victim and gradually tightening its coils until the prey is asphyxiated. The common Reticulated Python is known locally to exceed 5 metres in length, and is one of the world's largest snakes. This versatile species has adapted well to the urban environment, generally keeping well out of sight, and quietly feeding on sewer rats and stray cats.

One species of the family **Xenopeltidae**

is represented in Singapore. The Iridescent Earth Snake is most easily recognised by the intense iridescence (like a film of rainbow colours) which covers its entire body and is apparent under strong light. Under normal light, however, it appears uniformly brown above and white below. The head of this burrowing snake is relatively flat with small eyes.

Members of the family **Acrochordidae** are known as 'elephant trunk snakes', 'wart snakes' or 'file snakes'. They have rough baggy skin, small eyes set on smallish heads, and are almost entirely aquatic in habits, even giving birth to live young. The pointed tail of the Banded File Snake serves to distinguish it from the highly venomous sea-snakes which have a paddle-shaped tail. Although its movements are awkward on land, the Banded File Snake occasionally leaves the water and has been found hiding inside mud lobster mounds.

The family **Colubridae** is highly diverse in morphology and habits. Some groups are arboreal, others terrestrial, and even fossorial. Some, like the cat snakes of the genus *Boiga* are venomous, while others have surprising 'talents'. The Paradise Gliding Snake is able to distort its ventral surface into a concave shape and, using a typical sinuous snake-like motion while in mid-air, effectively glide from tree to tree. In addition to typical serpentine movements, a hitherto undocumented form of locomotion in snakes has twice been witnessed locally. When placed on a horizontal, slippery surface the diminutive Dwarf Reed Snake can contort itself into a hoop and successfully make a few rolls in an attempt to 'wheel' away. This remarkable behaviour deserves an in-depth study.

The family **Homalopsidae** comprises the 'mud snakes' which live partly or wholly in water. They are believed to be mildly venomous. While most species eat fish and swallow the prey whole, the Crab-eating Water Snake tightly grips a soft crab in its coils, and then rips bite-sized pieces off to swallow. To prevent sinking into soft mud, the mangrove-dwelling Dog-faced Water Snake moves effortlessly in a side-winding motion more typical of desert dwellers.

Keelbacks and mock-vipers belong to the family **Natricidae**. They generally have large eyes, and tend to be terrestrial or semi-aquatic in habits. Many species feed on fish and frogs, and some are known to be venomous.

The family **Pareatidae** is represented in Singapore by one introduced species, the White-spotted Slug Snake. These normally inoffensive snakes have blunt heads and feed largely on snails, slugs and earthworms. Fangs at the front of their lower jaws enable the snakes to extricate the soft parts of snails from their shells.

The families Homalopsidae, Natricidae and Pareatidae were, until recently, classified as subgroups in the Colubridae.

The family **Elapidae** consists of cobras, coral snakes and kraits. Elapids are reputed for their lethal venom, which can kill. The venom glands are linked to a pair of short, rigid fangs in the front of their upper jaws. Some of these snakes advertise their toxicity with bold patterning and bright colours.

The Blue Malayan Coral Snake is a startlingly beautiful creature. When resting on the dark forest floor its bright blue colour cannot be missed. Its cousin, the Banded Malayan Coral Snake, has a black and white banded underside and bright red tail to warn of its presence. Both species are mimicked by small harmless colubrid snakes and the Red-tailed Pipe Snake.

Cobras lack bright colours, but are famed for their ability to flatten and broaden their neck as an unmistakable warning display. The Equatorial Spitting Cobra can even spray venom from its fangs at the face of its tormentor, aiming directly for the eyes. The venom is supposed to cause extreme discomfort, and even temporary blindness, if it does actually get into the eyes.

Sea-snakes (family **Hydrophiidae**) are easily recognised by their short tails which are flattened into an oar-like paddle. While most are confined to the water throughout their lives, and bear live young underwater, the Amphibious Sea-snake leaves the water regularly, and lays eggs on dry land. It is thus, the only species of sea-snake featured in this book. Sea-snakes are generally regarded to be extremely venomous.

The vipers (family **Viperidae**) comprises a group of venomous snakes with triangular heads and short, thick bodies. Local vipers have a heat-sensitive pit between the eye and the nostril, used for detecting prey. They belong to the group known as 'pit-vipers'. Representative species in Singapore are arboreal and have prehensile tails. They are nocturnally active and are equipped with a pair of long fangs on the upper jaw to inject venom quickly and efficiently into both prey and predator. The venom of local pit-vipers is believed to be less lethal than that of elapid snakes.

## CROCODILES

(order Crocodylia) have a long snout,

short limbs with webbed feet, and a muscular, laterally compressed tail. Their large and powerful jaws are lined with conical teeth, and their body is covered in tough, leathery plate-like scales. Crocodiles are semi-aquatic predators of small animals. They lay their eggs on land, often in nests constructed of vegetation. The Estuarine Crocodile is the only species that is of confirmed occurrence in Singapore, and individuals measuring up to 2.5 metres or so are sometimes seen in the mangrove habitat.

## TURTLES (order

Testudines) are characterised by their body armour, which comprises an upper domed

shell or carapace, and a flat bony ventral plate or plastron enclosing its torso. When alarmed, the animal can withdraw its head, limbs and tail into its shell, thereby protecting its softer body parts. In members of the families **Geoemydidae** (formerly Bataguridae) and **Emydidae** the carapace and plastron are covered by an arrangement of hard rigid plates. We refer to these semi-aquatic animals as 'terrapins'. While the Geoemydidae are Asian turtles, the local representative of the Emydidae, the Red-eared Slider, is an introduced species from North America.

Members of the family **Trionychidae** are called 'soft-shelled turtles' as their carapace and plastron are covered with soft leathery skin. Due to their aquatic habits, these turtles have strongly webbed feet and a long, proboscis-like snout. They generally bury themselves in mud or leaf litter in shallow water in order to ambush their food, which comprises small creatures such as fishes or freshwater invertebrates, but they do sometimes leave the water to bask in the sun.

All turtles lay eggs, and even the fully aquatic marine turtles need to come ashore to do so. Marine turtles, characterised by their paddle-shaped limbs, are sighted sporadically in the sea around Singapore, but these are not covered in this book.

Despite considerable loss of natural habitats, Singapore's reptile fauna remains diverse. Although often unnecessarily killed, many snake species have adapted to life in urbanised areas. The uncommon and rare species of reptiles find a safe haven in the remaining patches of natural habitat that are protected as nature reserves. However, some species are still vulnerable to local extinction. The Estuarine Crocodile, for example, appear most at risk due to limited available habitat, high commercial value, and the danger that large individuals pose to humans.

Spotted House Gecko (*Gekko monarchus*) feeding on nectar of banana flower.
Chan Kwok Wai

## EARLESS AGAMID
*Aphaniotis fusca*

Kelvin Lim

Chan Kwok Wai

Squamata: Agamidae. To 22 cm TL. Body very slender with small scales, long slender limbs, long tail, relatively large angular head; largely hidden tympanum; and a small, low crest along the back. Brown, mature males have a blue iris, females have a white one. Largely arboreal, inhabiting tree trunks and shrubs in mature forest. It is diurnal and appears to feed largely on insects. In Singapore, occurs in the Central Nature Reserves. Distributed throughout the Malay Peninsula, Sumatra and Borneo.

## GREEN CRESTED LIZARD
*Bronchocela cristatella*

Nick Baker

Squamata: Agamidae. To 58 cm TL. Body moderately slender with small strongly keeled scales, head slender, long slender limbs and a very long tail. Spiny crest over middle of nape. Bright bluish-green (but may change to dark brown or grey) with blackish eye-ring and ear, rear part of tail dark brown. Diurnal and arboreal, this insectivorous lizard inhabits forest, scrubland and parkland. In Singapore, widespread in wooded areas. It used to be the common tree lizard in urban gardens, but has been largely displaced by the more aggressive Changeable Lizard. Distributed in southern Myanmar and Thailand, Peninsular Malaysia, Sumatra, Borneo, Java and the Philippines.

SBG, Hindhede Park 'o9; Feb; SBG Oct 'o9

# CHANGEABLE LIZARD
*Calotes versicolor*

Squamata: Agamidae. To 38 cm TL. Body robust with small strongly keeled scales, head large, long slender limbs and a long tail. A spiny crest along the middle of the nape and back. Two spines above the ear opening. Brownish to greenish yellow with blackish streaks radiating from the eyes, and brown bands along the back with a whitish stripe on the sides. Sexually dimorphic – adult males are larger with swollen cheeks, and develop orange heads with a black blotch over each cheek and throat during the breeding season. When displaying to females and rival males, the male performs a series of head nodding and push-ups. Diurnal and arboreal, it inhabits open areas such as scrubland and parkland, and sometimes forest clearings. It feeds on insects and even small lizards. In Singapore, this species first appeared in the 1980's and is believed to be introduced. It is presently common in urban parks and housing estates where it can be seen on tree trunks and fences. Native to India and Sri Lanka, southern China, and continental Southeast Asia as far south as the northern states of Peninsular Malaysia.

**Changeable Lizard male (left) and female**
Ft. Canning 2008; SBG Oct '09

# BLACK-BEARDED FLYING DRAGON
## *Draco melanopogon*

Squamata: Agamidae. To 24 cm TL. Body very slender with small scales and long slender limbs. A broad flap of skin (patagium) supported by ribs extending from the sides of its body. Topside of body olive or green with greyish brown bars or diamond-shaped blotches, patagium black with numerous yellow spots. Throat flap of males black and orange. Diurnal and arboreal, inhabiting trees in mature forest. It appears to feed largely on ants and other

small arthropods. Capable of gliding from tree to tree by extending the patagium at the sides of the body. In Singapore, occurs in the Central Nature Reserves. Distributed in the Malay Peninsula, Sumatra and Borneo.

---

# FIVE-BANDED FLYING DRAGON
## *Draco quinquefasciatus*

Squamata: Agamidae. To 27 cm TL. Body slender with small scales and long slender limbs. A broad flap of skin (patagium) supported by ribs extending from the sides of its body. Green mottled with brown on the body, patagium orange with five broad black bands. Throat flap orange and white. Diurnal and arboreal, inhabiting trees in mature forest. It appears to feed largely on ants and termites. Capable of gliding from tree to tree by

extending the patagium at the sides of the body. In Singapore, it was first recorded in 2001, and occurs only in the Central Nature Reserves. Distributed in the Malay Peninsula, Sumatra and Borneo.

# SUMATRAN FLYING DRAGON or COMMON FLYING DRAGON

*Draco sumatranus* (formerly confused with *Draco volans*)

Squamata: Agamidae. To 22 cm TL. Body slender with small scales and long slender limbs. A broad flap of skin (patagium) supported by ribs extending from the sides of its body. Topside of body light brown with dark brown blotches and whitish mottling, patagium black with irregular brownish and greenish blotches. The male has a bluish head and a large yellow throat flap. The female has a small, blue mottled throat flap. Diurnal and arboreal, inhabiting trees at forest edges, in parks and gardens, even in the city. Feeds largely on ants and termites. Capable of gliding from tree to tree by extending the patagium at the sides of the body. Widespread and common in Singapore, including offshore islands. Distributed in the Malay Peninsula, Sumatra, Borneo and Palawan.

Kelvin Lim

Nick Baker

**Displaying male and head of female (inset)**

SBG Oct '09; Singapore Zoo grounds '09    Mt. Faber
Fort Canning Oct '09

## KENDALL'S ROCK GECKO
*Cnemaspis kendallii*

Squamata: Gekkonidae. To about 14 cm TL. Skin relatively thin with small non-overlapping scales. Eyes large and without eyelids. Snout long, broad and slightly upturned; pupils distinctly rounded. Digits not expanded. Yellow above with dark brown and white blotches and streaks. Inhabits mature forest where it is both nocturnal and diurnal, and largely arboreal, frequenting tree trunks and large boulders. Tail is often held curled over its back. Regenerated tails tend to be yellow in colour. Apparently feeds largely on insects. In Singapore, known only from the Central Nature Reserves and Pulau Tekong. Distributed in the Malay Peninsula and Borneo.

Nick Baker

## FRILLY GECKO
*Cosymbotus craspedotus*

Squamata: Gekkonidae. To 12 cm TL. Skin relatively thin with small non-overlapping scales. Eyes large and without eyelids. Digits expanded into adhesive pads. Distinctly mottled with brown and grey above, yellowish below; a frill of skin on the sides of the body and the tail. Arboreal and nocturnal, probably feeding mainly on insects. The skin frills on the sides are not as effective for gliding as in the true gliding geckos (*Ptychozoon*), but help the animal blend into its surroundings by obliterating shadows. First reported from Singapore in 1992. Locally known from the Central Nature Reserves and Pulau Tekong. Occurs in the Malay Peninsula and Borneo.

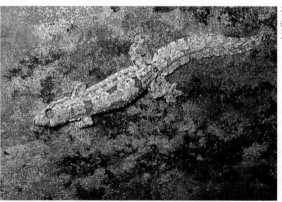

Lee King Ii

# FLAT-TAILED GECKO
## *Cosymbotus platyurus*

Squamata: Gekkonidae. To 12.5 cm TL. Skin relatively thin with small non-overlapping scales. Eyes large and without eyelids. Digits half-webbed and expanded into adhesive pads. Fringe of skin along sides of body, tail relatively flat with serrated margins. Colour variable, ranging from pale grey to grey with dark grey mottles and streaks. Nocturnal, arboreal and insectivorous, this species is commensal with humans. In Singapore, it is common and found in both wooded areas and in buildings. Widely distributed in tropical Asia.

Chan Kwok Wai

# PETER'S BENT-TOED GECKO
## *Cyrtodactylus consobrinus*

Squamata: Gekkonidae. To 28 cm TL. Skin relatively thin with small non-overlapping scales. Eyes large and without eyelids. Body black or brownish above with irregular white bands and reticulation. Digits not expanded. Inhabits mature forest where it frequents tree trunks and large boulders. It emerges at night to hunt for insects and other small animals. In Singapore, known only from the Bukit Timah Nature Reserve. The species occurs in the Malay Peninsula, Borneo and Sumatra.

## MALAYAN MARBLED BENT-TOED GECKO
*Cyrtodactylus quadrivirgatus*

Squamata: Gekkonidae. To 14 cm TL. Skin relatively thin with small non-overlapping scales. Eyes large and without eyelids. Digits not expanded. Body pinkish grey with two rows of blackish blotches down the back, tail blackish with whitish bands. Nocturnal, and arboreal on shrubs and tree trunks. This insectivorous lizard inhabits mature forest, and is confined to the Central Nature Reserves and Pulau Tekong in Singapore. Distributed in the Malay Peninsula, Sumatra and Borneo. *Cyrtodactylus quadrivirgatus* may not be the correct name for the Singapore

Chan Kwok Wai

## FOUR-CLAWED GECKO
*Gehyra mutilata*

Squamata: Gekkonidae. To 12 cm TL. Skin relatively thin with small non-overlapping scales. Eyes large and without eyelids. Digits expanded into adhesive pads, only four digits on fore foot have claws. Translucent pinkish brown with gold and blackish flecks. Tail smooth. Nocturnal, arboreal and insectivorous, this gecko is a human commensal, frequenting wooded areas as well as human habitations. Common in Singapore, and widely distributed throughout Southeast Asia and Oceania.

# SPOTTED HOUSE GECKO
## *Gekko monarchus*

Squamata: Gekkonidae. To 22 cm TL. Skin relatively thin with small non-overlapping scales. Eyes large and without eyelids. Digits expanded into adhesive pads. Body relatively robust and covered with warts, pale greyish-brown with seven to nine pairs of blackish blotches along the back, and a series of blackish bars on the tail. Nocturnal, insectivorous and arboreal, it inhabits disturbed forest, scrubland and parkland. It is to a certain extent, commensal with humans and does occur in buildings. In wooded habitats, it is more likely to be found on concrete structures, such as drain culverts. Widespread in Singapore, but more common in suburban and rural areas. Distributed in the Malay Peninsula, Sumatra, Borneo, Java, to the Philippines.

Nick Baker

# SPINY-TAILED HOUSE GECKO or COMMON HOUSE GECKO
## *Hemidactylus frenatus*

Squamata: Gekkonidae. To 13 cm TL. Skin relatively thin with small non-overlapping scales. Eyes large and without eyelids. Digits expanded into adhesive pads. Tail with longitudinal series of spiky tubercles. Colour variable, but tends to be pale greyish-brown with irregular dark grey streaks and mottles. Nocturnal and diurnal, arboreal and insectivorous, this species is commensal with humans. It is common in Singapore, frequenting both wooded areas and buildings. Widely distributed in tropical Asia.

Kelvin Lim

Nick Baker

**Mating pair**

## LOWLAND DWARF GECKO
*Hemiphyllodactylus typus*

Squamata: Gekkonidae. To 10 cm TL. Skin relatively thin with small non-overlapping scales. Eyes large and without eyelids. Digits expanded into adhesive pads. Body very slender with short limbs and prehensile tail. Body brown above with blackish markings over the back. Tail slender, pale brown or yellow with a yellowish blotch at the base. Nocturnal and arboreal, it inhabits shrubs and small trees in forest, scrubland and mangroves, and feeds on small insects. In Singapore, recorded from the Central Nature Reserves, the Western Catchment Area and Mandai Mangroves. Widely distributed throughout Southeast Asia and the Pacific Islands.

Norman Lim

## MOURNING GECKO or MARITIME GECKO
*Lepidodactylus lugubris*

Squamata: Gekkonidae. To 10 cm TL. Skin relatively thin with small non-overlapping scales. Eyes large and without eyelids. Digits expanded into adhesive pads. Body slender, greyish-brown with black flecks and densely frosted with white. A pair of elongated black spots on the nape. Top of broad tail with a series of irregular black-edged yellowish bands. Nocturnal and arboreal, it inhabits scrubland, coastal forest and mangroves. It is also commensal with humans to a certain extent, and can be found in buildings, although much more rarely than the other house-dwelling geckos. This is an all-female species that reproduces by parthenogenesis. Widespread throughout Singapore and apparently more common in coastal habitats. Distributed from Sri Lanka and the Maldives, and southern China, throughout Southeast Asia, New Guinea and the tropical South Pacific islands.

Nick Baker

## BROWN'S FLAP-LEGGED GECKO
*Luperosaurus browni*

Squamata: Gekkonidae. To 6.6 cm SV. Skin relatively thin with small non-overlapping scales. Eyes large and without eyelids. Digits expanded into adhesive pads. Body long and slender, mottled with brown, grey and white, with five irregular dark-brown cross-bars over the dorsum. Digits half-webbed; flaps of skin present along the sides of the limbs, but absent on the sides of the body; tail serrated on the sides. Inhabits forest, living on shrubs and tree trunks. This nocturnal animal probably feeds largely on insects. In Singapore, known only from Pulau Tekong where it was first discovered in August 2005. Occurs in the Malay Peninsula and Borneo.

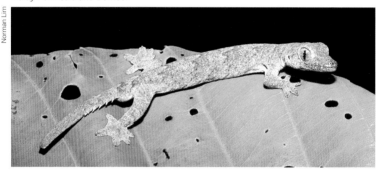

Norman Lim

## KUHL'S GLIDING GECKO
*Ptychozoon kuhli*

Norman Lim

Squamata: Gekkonidae. To 19 cm TL. Skin relatively thin with small non-overlapping scales. Eyes large and without eyelids. Digits expanded into adhesive pads. Body mottled with brown, grey, white and black. A wide flap of skin along the sides, limbs and neck; tail with a fringe of lappets on the sides, ending in a large flap at the tip. Inhabits forest, living on trees where it is well-camouflaged against the bark. This nocturnal animal feeds on insects, and is capable of making glides over short distances with the large flaps of skin on its sides. In Singapore, known only from Pulau Tekong where it was first discovered in 2002. Occurs in the Malay Peninsula, Sumatra, Borneo and Java.

## BROWN TREE SKINK
*Dasia grisea*

Squamata: Scincidae. To about 28 cm TL. Body robust, covered in shiny strongly keeled, overlapping scales; symmetrical arrangement of large scales on top of the head. Body olive brown above with a series of irregular and narrow black bands and white spots. Hatchlings with black and yellowish bands over the back, and tail yellow with narrow black bands. In Singapore, inhabits mature forest where it is largely arboreal and diurnal in habits, and feeds mainly on small invertebrates. It gives birth to live young. In Singapore, inhabits the Central Nature Reserves. Occurs in southern Thailand down the Malay Peninsula to Singapore, Borneo, Sumatra and the Philippines. First recorded in Singapore in 1998.

Nick Baker

## OLIVE TREE SKINK
*Dasia olivacea*

Squamata: Scincidae. To 27 cm TL. Body robust, covered in weakly keeled overlapping scales, symmetrical arrangement of large scales on top of the head. Body olive above with a series of whitish spots with blackish edges, bright green below. Hatchlings black above with narrow red bands and a uniformly red tail, the red gradually changes into yellow and green with growth. In Singapore, inhabits mature inland and coastal forest where it is largely arboreal and diurnal in habits, and feeds mainly on small invertebrates. It gives birth to live young. Rare in Singapore. Recently reported from the Central Nature Reserves and Pulau Ubin. Occurs in southern Thailand down the Malay Peninsula to Singapore, Borneo, Sumatra and Java.

Nick Baker

**Juvenile**

## STRIPED TREE SKINK
*Lipinia vittigera*

Squamata: Scincidae. To 10 cm TL. Body slender and covered in shiny smooth, overlapping scales; symmetrical arrangement of large scales on top of the head; snout elongated. Body and head with a broad yellow stripe bordered by a black stripe on either margin along the back; tail long and orange. Inhabits mature forest where it is largely arboreal and diurnal in habits, and feeds on small invertebrates. In Singapore, found uncommonly in the Central Nature Reserves. It is widely distributed in continental Southeast Asia, Sumatra and Borneo.

## GARDEN SUPPLE SKINK
*Lygosoma bowringii* (formerly as *Riopa bowringii*)

Squamata: Scincidae. To 11 cm TL. Body very slender, covered in shiny smooth or weakly keeled overlapping scales, symmetrical arrangement of large scales on top of the head. Limbs very small, tail long but relatively thick. Body bronze-brown on the back bordered by a yellowish stripe on each side. Sides blackish with white spots and a red patch behind the arm. Belly bright yellow. This small, worm-like lizard is terrestrial and semi-fossorial

with diurnal habits, and feeds on small soil invertebrates. It seems to be commensal with humans, being largely found in habitats disturbed by human activities. Common and widespread in Singapore in urban gardens and lawns. Widespread in Southeast Asia.

## MANGROVE SKINK
*Emoia atrocostata*

Squamata: Scincidae. To 26 cm TL. Body moderately slender, covered in overlapping smooth scales, symmetrical arrangement of large scales on top of the head. Greyish brown along the back, bluish with a blackish stripe along the sides. The topside, tail and limbs are covered with whitish spots. Some individuals have orange bellies. Diurnal, largely terrestrial and semi-arboreal, and inhabits coastal habitats such as rocky beaches and mangroves. It feeds largely on insects and small crustaceans. In Singapore, it appears to be rare but there is a thriving population at the Sungei Buloh Wetland Reserve. Distributed throughout insular Southeast Asia and tropical western Pacific.

Nick Baker

## STRIPED SUN SKINK or ROUGH-SCALED SKINK
*Eutropis rugiferus* (formerly as *Mabuya rugifera*)

Squamata: Scincidae. To 18 cm TL. Body robust, covered in overlapping and strongly keeled scales, symmetrical arrangement of large scales on top of the head. Body brown or olive-green above usually with 5 to 7 yellowish stripes or series of spots, greenish-white below. Inhabits mature forest where it is largely terrestrial, partially arboreal and diurnal in habits, and feeds mainly on small invertebrates. In Singapore, found uncommonly in the Central Nature Reserves. Occurs in the Malay Peninsula, Borneo, Sumatra and Java.

Norman Lim

# COMMON SUN SKINK or MANY-LINED SUN SKINK
*Eutropis multifasciatus* (formerly as *Mabuya multifasciata*)

Squamata: Scincidae. To 35 cm TL. Body robust, covered in shiny overlapping and strongly keeled scales, symmetrical arrangement of large scales on top of the head. Body bronze-brown with or without a series of thin black stripes down the back. Sides either blackish with white spots or with a swathe of orange from the ear to the hind legs. Underside of the head yellow on some individuals. Inhabits forest, mangroves and scrubland where it is diurnal and mainly terrestrial in habits. It feeds mainly on insects and bears live young. In Singapore, widespread in wooded areas, mangroves and parkland. Distributed from southern China and north-eastern India, and throughout Southeast Asia. SBG Oct.09

**Juvenile**

# CLOUDED MONITOR
## *Varanus nebulosus* (also as *Varanus bengalensis nebulosus*)

Squamata: Varanidae. To 1.7 m TL. Large and robust, skin thick and leathery with small non-overlapping scales. Tongue slender and forked. Snout relatively short with nostrils positioned midway between the eye and the tip of the snout. Greyish brown densely covered with yellow spots. Inhabits mature forest and adjacent parkland, where it is diurnal and both terrestrial and arboreal. It feeds on small animals which it often searches for by digging in the substrate. In Singapore, it is found in the Central Nature Reserves, Bukit Batok Nature Park, Pulau Ubin and Pulau Tekong. Its population in Singapore appears to be increasing. Distributed in continental Southeast Asia and Java.

Nick Bakar

**Adult (bottom) and juvenile**

Chan Kwok Wai

Bukit Timah          Singapore Zoo grounds & Bukit Timah Cet.

# MALAYAN WATER MONITOR
*Varanus salvator*

Squamata: Varanidae. To 3 m TL, this is among the largest lizards in the world. Large and robust, skin thick and leathery with small non-overlapping scales. Tongue slender and forked. Snout long and slender, with nostrils positioned close to the tip. Hatchlings are black with whitish undersides and rows of bright yellow spots forming bands along the back and tail. This colour pattern fades as it grows and large adults are often plain grey-ish-brown. Inhabits forest, mangroves, scrubland and beaches where it tends to stay close to water bodies. Mainly terrestrial, but also climbs trees (where it commonly spends the night) and is an expert swimmer and diver. This diurnal creature feeds on small animals and fish, as well as scavenges on carrion and kitchen waste. In Singapore, widespread and often encountered along large canals in the city area. Distributed from Sri Lanka and southern China, and throughout Southeast Asia.

Nick Baker

**Adult (above) and juvenile**

Kelvin Lim

SBG — near Symphony Lake F:1'09; Oct,'09
Sungei Buloh

## BRAHMINY BLIND SNAKE
*Ramphotyphlops braminus*

Nick Baker

Squamata: Typhlopidae. To 18 cm TL. Small, cylindrical, smooth and entirely black except for the extremities which are whitish. Head rounded with tiny black eyes, tail very short and knobby with a short and rigid spine. Can be mistaken for an earthworm, but is not slimy, lacks rings on the body and has a tongue that sticks out occasionally. Fossorial and most likely to be seen under rocks and logs, sometimes even in flower pots. Feeds on tiny soil-dwelling invertebrates such as the larvae of ants and termites. Apparently an all-female species that lays eggs. Harmless to humans. Common in Singapore where it is usually found in gardens. Widespread in Asia and Africa, Oceania and North and Central America, largely in the tropics.

## WHITE-BELLIED BLIND SNAKE
*Typhlops muelleri*

Robert Teo

Squamata: Typhlopidae. To 45 cm TL. Body thick, cylindrical, blackish brown above and white below with a sharp line of demarcation between colours on the sides. Head round with small black eyes, tail very short and knobby with a short and rigid spine. Fossorial, usually occurring in forest and scrubland. Feeds on soil-dwelling invertebrates and is oviparous. Nonvenomous. Uncommon in Singapore where it has been recorded from the Central Nature Reserves and Pulau Ubin. Distributed in the Malay Peninsula, Sumatra and Borneo.

# RETICULATED PYTHON
## *Python reticulatus*

Squamata: Pythonidae. To just under 10 m TL, but Singapore specimens rarely exceed 5 m TL. Body thick-set, scales smooth and iridescent, head distinct with heat-sensing pits along the lips, eye orange with vertically elliptical pupil. Greyish brown above and on sides with a network of irregular black lines, white on underside. White spots along sides at intersections of black lines, a black line down middle of the head, and an oblique black line from hind corner of eye towards neck. This snake is both terrestrial and arboreal. It is also an excellent swimmer. It is oviparous, nocturnal and feeds on small mammals and birds. A constrictor, it kills its prey by coiling around it and squeezing it out of breath. Common in Singapore and found in most habitats from forest to mangroves, and often near human habitation. Although non-venomous, large individuals are potentially dangerous as they are capable of overpowering a person. This is one of the largest snakes in the world. Widespread in Southeast Asia.

Norman Lim

# SUNBEAM SNAKE or IRIDESCENT EARTH SNAKE
*Xenopeltis unicolor*

Squamata: Xenopeltidae. To 114 cm TL. Body thick-set, brown on the topside, white on the underside, and covered with smooth and highly iridescent scales. Head depressed and not distinct from body, tail short but tapering. Hatchlings have a white bar across the back of the neck. Semi-fossorial and nocturnal in habits, it is found in forest, scrubland and rural areas. It is known to feed on rats, birds, lizards and other snakes, and is oviparous. Non-venomous. Common in Singapore, and also found on Pulau Ubin and Pulau Tekong. Distributed throughout Southeast Asia.

Chan Kwok Wai

# BANDED FILE SNAKE
*Acrochordus granulatus*

Squamata: Acrochordidae. To 1 m TL. Skin loosely hanging and covered with small rough scales. Head not distinct from body, tail tapering and slightly compressed. Body with black and white bands throughout. Its colour pattern is similar to that of venomous sea-snakes, but the file snake's tail tapers to a point, and not oar-shaped. Mostly aquatic and nocturnal, it feeds on small fish, and gives birth to live young. It occurs in the sea usually in and around river mouths. During low tide, it has been found out of water, concealed inside mud-lobster mounds. Non-venomous. In Singapore, it seems to be uncommon, and is usually recorded from the Johor Straits, including Sungei Buloh Wetland Reserve. Distributed in the eastern Indian Ocean and the western Pacific from Hainan and the Philippines to northern Australia.

Ria Tan

# ORIENTAL WHIP SNAKE
## *Ahaetulla prasina*

Squamata: Colubridae. To 1.9 m TL. Head distinct from very slender body, snout pointed in side profile. Pupil of eye horizontally elongated. Adults bright fluorescent green above, juveniles yellow to pale brown. Snout twice as long as the width of the eye. Ventrum pale green with a pair of yellow stripes. Arboreal and diurnal, inhabits forest edge, scrubland and gardens. Known to feed on lizards, frogs and small birds. Gives birth to live young. Mildly venomous, but usually not aggressive. Occurs throughout Singapore in wooded areas, and suburban parks and gardens. Widely distributed from eastern India, Myanmar, southern China, Thailand and Indochina, the Philippines, southwards through the Malay Peninsula, Sumatra, Borneo, Java and Sulawesi.

Chan Kwok Wai

Joe Lim

**Adult (above) and juvenile**

# BIGEYE GREEN WHIP SNAKE or MALAYAN WHIP SNAKE
## *Ahaetulla mycterizans*

Squamata: Colubridae. To 1 m TL. Head distinct from very slender body, snout pointed in side profile. Pupil of eye horizontally elongated. Lime green above. Snout as long as, or 1.5 times the width of the eye. Ventrum white with three green stripes. Arboreal and diurnal, inhabits the forest interior, and usually on vegetation overhanging streams. Probably feeds on lizards. Mildly venomous. In Singapore, confined to the Central Nature Reserves. Distributed in the Malay Peninsula, Sumatra and Java.

Ria Tan

# DOG-TOOTHED CAT SNAKE
## *Boiga cynodon*

Squamata: Colubridae. To 2.7 m TL. Head distinct from body. Body very slender, laterally compressed; usually yellowish or brown with irregular black cross bars, some snakes are almost entirely black; head light brown with a black streak behind the eye; pupils elliptical.

Occurs mainly in mature forest where it is mainly arboreal and mainly nocturnal, and preys mainly on birds, their eggs, and small mammals. The species has a mildly venomous bite. In Singapore, known from the Central Catchment Nature Reserve, Pulau Ubin and Pulau Tekong. It ranges over much of Southeast Asia.

Chua Ee Kiam

# GOLD-RINGED CAT SNAKE or MANGROVE SNAKE
*Boiga dendrophila*

Squamata: Colubridae. To 2.5 m TL. Head distinct from body. Body shiny black with a seies of 40 to 50 narrow bright yellow bands. In the local form (the subspecies *B. dendrophila melanota*), these bands do not meet over the back. Throat and lips yellow. Inhabits mature inland forest and mangroves where it is nocturnal and largely arboreal, although it is often encountered swimming in pools and streams. It feeds on lizards, birds and small mam-

mals. Mildly venomous. In Singapore, recorded mainly from the Central Catchment Nature Reserve. Distributed in the Malay Peninsula, Borneo, Sumatra, Java, Sulawesi and the Philippines.

# JASPER CAT SNAKE
*Boiga jaspidea*

Squamata: Colubridae. To 1.4 m TL. Head distinct from body. Body very slender, laterally compressed; greyish-brown above speckled with black and pink, throat and fore-part of belly yellow; scales on mid-dorsum enlarged; pupils elliptical. Occurs in mature forest where it is primarily arboreal and nocturnal, and is known to feed on small mice. It appears to be mildly venomous. In Singapore, known from the Central Catchment Nature Reserve and Pulau Tekong. Distributed in the Malay Peninsula, Sumatra, Borneo and Java.

# VARIABLE REED SNAKE
## *Calamaria lumbricoidea*

Squamata: Colubridae. To 50 cm TL. Body cylindrical, head hardly distinct from body, tail relatively short, dorsal scales smooth. Body uniformly dark brown above with a white or yellow stripe along the side. Underside with black and yellowish white bands. Hatchlings have a pink head and may be confused with the Pink-headed Reed Snake. However, they have narrow whitish bands over the back, and the underside is banded. Inhabits mature forest where it lives on the ground among leaf litter. It is nocturnal and reported to feed on small lizards, frogs and earthworms. Not known to be venomous. In Singapore, confined to the Central Nature Reserves. Distributed in the Malay Peninsula, Borneo, Sumatra, Java and the Philippines.

Alan Yeo

# PINK-HEADED REED SNAKE
## *Calamaria schlegeli*

Squamata: Colubridae. To 40 cm TL. Body cylindrical, head hardly distinct from body, tail relatively short, dorsal scales smooth. Head bright pink, body and tail black above and uniformly white below. Inhabits mature forest where it lives on the ground among the leaf litter. It is nocturnal and probably feeds on small invertebrates and lizards. Not known to be venomous, its bright colouration apparently mimics that of the Blue Malayan Coral Snake. However, it lacks the blue stripe on the sides and the red tail. In Singapore, known from the Central Nature Reserves and Ulu Pandan. Distributed in the Malay Peninsula, Borneo, Sumatra and Java.

Norman Lim

# PARADISE GLIDING SNAKE or PARADISE TREE SNAKE
*Chrysopelea paradisi*

Squamata: Colubridae. To 1.3 m TL. Body slender and cylindrical, head relatively flat and distinct from body. Black above with a green or yellow spot on each dorsal scale. Some individuals have a row of red 'flower' pattern (groups of four red spots) along the middle of the back. Underside yellowish green. Top of head and snout with five yellow bands. Mildly venomous. This diurnal, oviparous and arboreal snake feeds mainly on lizards and small birds. It is able to glide by launching into the air and flattening its body, drawing in its ventrum. In Singapore, it is common and recorded all over the main island, and on surrounding islands, in forest, scrubland, mangroves and even in urban gardens. Distributed in the Malay Peninsula, Borneo, Sumatra, Java, Sulawesi and the Philippines.

## TWIN-BARRED GLIDING SNAKE or TWIN-BARRED TREE SNAKE
*Chrysopelea pelias*

Chan Kwok Wai

Squamata: Colubridae. To 74 cm TL. Body slender and cylindrical, head relatively flat and distinct from body. Grey above with series of broad, red saddles on back; each saddle separated by narrow, black edged whitish band. Occurs in forest where it is mainly arboreal and diurnal, and feeds on lizards. This back-fanged snake is mildly venomous. Very little else known of its habits, but it is probably able to glide like its common relative, the Paradise Gliding Snake. In Singapore, it occurs mainly in the Central Catchment Nature Reserve, with isolated reports from other forested parts of the island and Pulau Ubin. Distributed in the Malay Peninsula, Borneo, Sumatra and Java.

## COMMON MALAYAN RACER
*Coelognathus flavolineatus* (formerly as *Elaphe flavolineata*)

Squamata: Colubridae. To 180 cm TL. Head distinct from long and cylindrical body. Blackish brown with a series of black blotches on the sides along the front part of the body. A broad black-edged, yellowish brown stripe down the middle of the back which darkens out over the rear part. Head with two short black streaks behind and below eye, and an oblique black stripe along the neck, lips whitish. Inhabits forest, scrubland and rural areas; this largely terrestrial, oviparous and apparently diurnal species feeds on small vertebrates (e.g. rats) which it kills by constriction. It seems to be non-venomous. In Singapore, uncommon but widespread. Distributed in Myanmar, Thailand, the Malay Peninsula, Borneo, Sumatra and Java.

Norman Lim

## ELEGANT BRONZEBACK
*Dendrelaphis formosus* (formerly confused with *Dendrelaphis cyanochloris*)

Squamata: Colubridae. To about 1.4 m TL. Head distinct from slender body, eye large. Scales along middle of back distinctly enlarged. Bronze brown above, a broad black stripe on the side of the head and neck. Side of neck with blue skin between the scales. Underside yellowish green. Rear part of body with three black lines and a pale whitish stripe on each side. Inhabits mature forest, is diurnal, arboreal, oviparous, and probably eats lizards and frogs. Apparently non-venomous. In Singapore, it is confined to the Central Nature Reserves. The Elegant Bronzeback is distributed in the Malay Peninsula, Sumatra, Borneo and Java.

This snake (below), photographed in the Central Nature Reserve, is tentatively identified as the **Blue Bronzeback** (*Dendrelaphis cyanochloris*) because the neck has blue skin between the scales, and it does not appear to have three black lines along the rear part of the body. The latter character distinguishes it from the Elegant Bronzeback. The Blue Bronzeback is distributed from India to Thailand and possibly occurs in the Malay Peninsula. We hesitate to confirm the occurrence of the Blue Bronzeback in Singapore based solely on this photograph.

## STRIPED BRONZEBACK
*Dendrelaphis caudolineatus*

Squamata: Colubridae. To 1.5 m TL. Head distinct from slender body, eye large. Scales along middle of back not enlarged. Head brown above, lips yellowish. Body brown above with six narrow black stripes from neck down the back and tail. Sides of body with a white stripe and a black stripe below that. Underside greenish yellow with a black stripe under the tail. Arboreal, diurnal, oviparous, and feeds on lizards and frogs. It inhabits forest, scrubland and gardens. Apparently non-venomous. In Singapore, it is widespread in suburban and rural areas. Distributed in the Malay Peninsula, Borneo, Sumatra, Java and the Philippines.

Norman Lim

## RED-NECKED BRONZEBACK or KOPSTEIN'S BRONZEBACK
*Dendrelaphis kopsteini* (formerly confused with *Dendrelaphis formosus*)

Squamata: Colubridae. To about 1.4 m TL. Head distinct from slender body, eye large. Scales along middle of back distinctly enlarged. Bronze brown above, the neck region bright orange-red. A black streak on the side of the head and fore part of the neck. Underside yellowish green on the front half, and dull green to brown on the rear. Arboreal, diurnal, oviparous, feeds largely on lizards and frogs. Apparently non-venomous. Inhabits forest, scrubland and gardens. In Singapore, it is widespread in suburban and rural areas, and in the Central Nature Reserves. Distributed in the Malay Peninsula and Sumatra.

Norman Lim

# PAINTED BRONZEBACK
## *Dendrelaphis pictus*

Squamata: Colubridae. To about 1 m TL. Head distinct from slender body, eye large. Scales along middle of back distinctly enlarged. Body bronze brown above with a yellowish white stripe on the sides. A black stripe on the side of the head begins from the snout, passes through the eye, and continues over the top margin of the white stripe along the side of the body. A series of oblique black bands on the neck and forepart of the body, between which the skin is blue. Underside yellow or greenish. Arboreal, diurnal, oviparous and

feeds on lizards and frogs. It inhabits forest, scrubland and gardens. In Singapore, this apparently non-venomous snake is common in suburban and rural areas, and also on surrounding islands. Distributed in southern China and Indochina, the Malay Peninsula, Borneo, Sumatra, Java, Sulawesi, to Timor and the Philippines.

# MALAYAN BRIDLE SNAKE or SADDLED TREE SNAKE
## *Dryocalamus subannulatus*

Squamata: Colubridae. To 60 cm TL. Head distinct from body. Body very slender, light brown above with a series of dark brown saddle blotches; ventral scales keeled, dorsal scales smooth. Found in mature forest where it seems to be both arboreal and terrestrial, and nocturnal in habits. It is known to feed on lizards, and is apparently non-venomous. In Singapore, confined to the Central Nature Reserves. Occurs on the Malay Peninsula, Sumatra, Borneo and Palawan.

## KEEL-BELLIED WHIP SNAKE
*Dryophiops rubescens*

Squamata: Colubridae. To 1 m TL. Head distinct from slender body. Prominent ridge between the eye and the snout. Pupil of eye horizontally elongated. Body grey or reddish brown with a series of black spots along the middle of the back. Head with dark brown streaks on the top and on the side. Underside yellow, rear part mottled with brown. Has a distinct red tongue. Arboreal, diurnal, oviparous, and feeds on lizards and frogs. It seems to be mildly venomous, and inhabits mature forest. In Singapore, found in the Central Nature Reserves, and also on Pulau Ubin and Pulau Tekong. Distributed in the Malay Peninsula, Borneo, Sumatra, Java and the Philippines.

Norman Lim

## ORANGE-BELLIED RINGNECK
*Gongylosoma baliodeirum* (formerly as *Liopeltis baliodeira*)

Squamata: Colubridae. To about 35 cm TL. Body cylindrical with smooth dorsal scales. Dark brown above with yellow spots on neck and fore part of body; underside orange; dorsal scales smooth. Inhabits mature forest where it is mainly terrestrial, but known to climb shrubs. It seems to be non-venomous and probably feeds on lizards and insects. In Singapore, known from the Central Nature Reserves. Distributed in Indochina, the Malay Peninsula, Sumatra, Borneo and Java.

Benjamin Y H Lee

# RED-TAILED RACER
*Gonyosoma oxycephalum*

Daniel Koh

Squamata: Colubridae. To over 2.4 m TL. Head distinct from thick-set and laterally compressed body. Usually bright green above on head and body, paler green below; tail rusty brown; dorsal scales largely smooth. An unusual orange-coloured morph is illustrated here. Inhabits mature forest, being primarily arboreal and diurnal in habits, and feeds mainly on birds and small mammals. Apparently non-venomous. In Singapore, it is known from the Central Nature Reserves and Pulau Tekong. Widely distributed throughout Southeast Asia.

**Green morph (left) and orange morph**

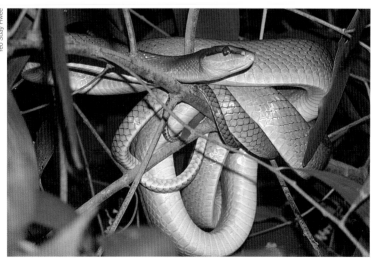

Teo Suay Hwee

## HOUSE WOLF SNAKE or COMMON WOLF SNAKE
*Lycodon capucinus* (formerly confused with *Lycodon aulicus*)

Norman Lim

Squamata: Colubridae. To 76 cm TL. Dark purplish brown above with numerous yellowish spots, and a broad yellowish collar. Head relatively flat, uniformly dark brown above. Lips yellowish, underside of body white. Body slender with smooth scales. Apparently commensal with humans and often encountered in buildings and in gardens. Arboreal and terrestrial in habits, this nocturnal and oviparous snake feeds largely on geckos. Many individuals are highly irritable and will bite readily when provoked, often vibrating the tip of its tail as a warning. Not known to be venomous. In Singapore and its larger surrounding islands, common in suburban and rural habitats. Occurs throughout Southeast Asia.

## BANDED WOLF SNAKE
*Lycodon subcinctus*

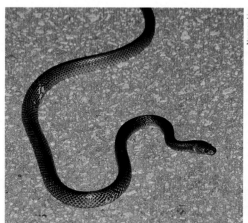

Norman Lim

Squamata: Colubridae. To 100 cm TL. Body dark-brown or black with widely-spaced white bands on the front portion, and which darken progressively over the posterior end. Young examples have 20 white bands throughout the body, but these bands become very faint in larger specimens. Head relatively flat, body scales smooth. Inhabits mature forest where it appears to be nocturnal and primarily terrestrial. It feeds mainly on lizards and appears to be non-venomous. In Singapore, known from only two specimens: one in the Central Catchment Nature Reserve in 1988, the other (shown here) from Pulau Tekong in 2006. It occurs over most of Southeast Asia.

# BROWN KUKRI SNAKE
*Oligodon purpurascens*

Squamata: Colubridae. To 95 cm TL. Head not distinct from thick-set body, dorsal scales smooth. Purplish brown above with a series of widely spaced dark-brown or grey, black-edged saddle blotches down the back; and two or three narrow irregular black bars between the blotches. A dark brown chevron band across the nape, its apex reaching to top of head between the eyes; and a broad dark brown band across the snout between the eyes. Underside pink, bright red in juveniles. There is a distinct colour form that is red with narrow black-edged pale brown bars or oval blotches over the back. Semi-fossorial, nocturnal and oviparous. This inhabitant of mature forest is known to feed on bird's eggs, and seems to be non-venomous. In Singapore, restricted to the Central Nature Reserves. Distributed in the Malay Peninsula, Sumatra, Borneo and Java. The red form is known from southern Peninsular Malaysia, Pulau Tioman and Singapore.

Gloria Seow

The **Barred Kukri Snake** (*Oligodon signatus*), not illustrated here, also occurs in the Central Nature Reserves. Its colour pattern resembles the red form of the Brown Kukri Snake, but is dark brown with narrow red bands, the first two or three of which are chevron shaped with their apex pointing towards the head. It grows to about 60 cm TL.

**Red morph (left) and brown morph**

Tsang Kwok Choong

# STRIPED KUKRI SNAKE
## *Oligodon octolineatus*

Norman Lim

Squamata: Colubridae. To 68 cm TL. Head not distinct from thick-set body, dorsal scales smooth. Greyish brown above with a vermillion stripe down the middle of the back. This stripe is flanked by three black stripes on each side. An oblique black band on the side of the head, and a black band over the top of the snout between the eyes. Underside pink. This semi-fossorial snake is nocturnal and oviparous, and frequents forest, scrubland and gardens. It is known to eat lizards, other snakes and bird's eggs. Its striking dorsal colour pattern appears to mimic that of the highly venomous Banded Malayan Coral Snake, but it is apparently not venomous. In Singapore, it is present throughout the main island in suburban areas, and is also found on Pulau Ubin and Pulau Tekong. Distributed in the Malay Peninsula, Sumatra, Borneo and Java.

SBG

# DWARF REED SNAKE
## *Pseudorabdion longiceps*

Norman Lim

Squamata: Colubridae. To 23 cm TL. Body cylindrical, head hardly distinct from body, tail relatively short, dorsal scales smooth. Snout distinctly pointed. Wholly iridescent black, some individuals have a narrow pale yellow collar and a pair of yellow spots on the nape. Inhabits forest and scrubland where it lives on the ground among the leaf litter. It appears to be non-venomous and nocturnal, and is known to feed on insects. In Singapore, the species has twice been observed curling its body into a rigid circle, and rolling in a hoop-like manner two or three times. Distributed in the Malay Peninsula, Sumatra, Borneo and Sulawesi. In Singapore, known mainly from the Central Nature Reserves and also on Pulau Tekong.

# KEELED RAT SNAKE
*Ptyas carinata* (formerly as *Zaocys carinatus*)

Squamata: Colubridae. To 4 m TL. Head distinct from slender and thick-set body which is triangular in cross section. Two rows of dorsal scales along back keeled. Brown to blackish on the front part of the body with or without yellow bands. Rear half of body yellowish brown with a distinct black net pattern, tail black with yellow spots. Side of head and throat whitish, belly blackish. Largely inhabits forest and feeds on small vertebrates. It appears to be non-venomous. Oviparous, diurnal and mainly terrestrial in habits. In Singapore, uncommon and recorded from the Central Nature Reserves. Widely distributed in Southeast Asia.

Nick Baker

# WHITE-BELLIED RAT SNAKE
*Ptyas fusca* (formerly as *Zaocys fuscus*)

Squamata: Colubridae. To 2.9 m TL. Head distinct from slender body with smooth dorsal scales. Brown above with a reddish brown stripe along the middle of the back on the rear part of the body and tail. A broad black stripe along the sides at rear part of body and tail. Underside yellowish or white. This terrestrial, oviparous and diurnal species inhabits mature forest and is often found near and in water. It feeds on lizards and rats, and appears to be non-venomous. In Singapore, recorded only from the Central Nature Reserves. Distributed in the Malay Peninsula, Borneo and Sumatra.

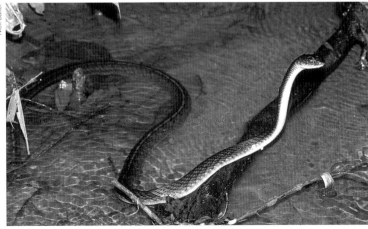

Nick Baker

## BLACK-HEADED COLLARED SNAKE
### *Sibynophis melanocephalus*

Squamata: Colubridae. To 60 cm TL. Body dark brown on back with a pair of pale brown stripes, each stripe with a series of black spots or bands. Head relatively flat, black or reddish brown, densely speckled with white except for the nape; lips whitish. Body slender with smooth scales. Terrestrial, oviparous and apparently diurnal in habits. Known to feed on lizards, frogs and insects. Inhabits forest and scrubland. Not known to be venomous. In Singapore, known from the Central Catchment Nature Reserve, the Western Catchment Area and Pulau Tekong. Distributed in the Malay Peninsula, Sumatra and Borneo.

Chua Siew Chin

## MALAYAN BROWN SNAKE
### *Xenelaphis hexagonotus*

Squamata: Colubridae. To 2 m TL. Head distinct from thick-set body, dorsal scales smooth. Dark brown above and white to yellow below, with a series of narrow black bars on the side of the body in the anterior part. Inhabits mature forest, particularly in freshwater swamps, where it seems to be largely ter-restrial but enters water freely. Diurnal, oviparous, and apparently non-venom-ous, it preys on rats and fish. In Singapore, it is recorded from the Central Catchment Nature Reserve and Pulau Ubin. Distributed in the Malay Peninsula, Sumatra, Borneo and Java.

Nick Baker

# CANTOR'S WATER SNAKE
*Cantoria violacea*

Chan Kwok Wai

Squamata: Homalopsidae. To about 1.2 m TL. Body very slender, yellow with thick black or brown saddle blotches throughout; some individuals have the rear half of the body almost entirely black. Tail tapering and pointed. Inhabits mangroves, being largely aquatic and primarily nocturnal in habits. It is known to feed on snapping shrimps. The colour pattern of this mildly venomous species strongly resembles that of some sea-snakes, but it lacks the flat, paddle-shaped tail of its highly venomous relatives. In Singapore, known from mangrove areas at Pasir Ris, Lim Chu Kang and Sungei Buloh Wetland Reserve. Distributed along the coasts of Myanmar and the Andaman Islands, the Malay Peninsula, Sumatra and Borneo.

# DOG-FACED WATER SNAKE
*Cerberus rynchops*

Squamata: Homalopsidae. To 1 m TL. Eyes small and situated on top of head close to snout. Head distinct from body, with oblique black stripe at rear eye margin. Body olive grey above with irregular narrow blackish bars and spots, scales strongly keeled. Underside

Nick Baker

yellow mottled with black. Nocturnal, primarily aquatic, and feeds on small fish. Gives birth to live young. Known to be mildly venomous. Occurs in estuarine areas, especially in mangroves, and also in canals in built-up areas. In Singapore, common all along the coast. Widely distributed in tropical Indo-west Pacific.

## CRAB-EATING WATER SNAKE
*Fordonia leucobalia*

Squamata: Homalopsidae. To 94 cm TL. Head rounded, not distinct from body. Body cylindrical, thick-set with relatively short tail. Scales smooth. Dark purplish brown above fading to white on the underside. Nocturnal, semi-aquatic, ovo-viviparous, and feeds on hard-shelled crabs. Known to be mildly venomous. Occurs mainly in mangroves. In Singapore, known mainly from estuaries along the northern coast, including Sungei Buloh and Pasir Ris. Distributed along the coast of Indochina, Malaysia, Indonesia to northern Australia.

Chan Kwok Wai

## YELLOW-LIPPED WATER SNAKE or GERARD'S WATER SNAKE
*Gerarda prevostiana*

Squamata: Homalopsidae. To 53 cm TL. Head rounded, slightly distinct from body. Body cylindrical, grey above, pale brown below with a blackish stripe along the middle. Upper lips yellow, extending to a yellow stripe along side of body. Scales smooth. Nocturnal, semi-aquatic, ovo-viviparous and feeds on newly moulted (soft-shelled) crabs. Mildly venomous. Occurs in mangroves. In Singapore, known from estuarine areas along the northern coast, including Sungei Buloh and Pasir Ris. Distributed along the coast of India east to the Malacca Straits.

Chan Kwok Wai

# PUFF-FACED WATER SNAKE
## Homalopsis buccata

Squamata: Homalopsidae. To 1.2 m TL. Head broad, distinct from body. Snout black, an oblique black stripe across the eye. Body thick-set and cylindrical, grey with black-edged dark brown rectangular saddles along back. In hatchlings, the back is orange while the saddles are black. Scales keeled. Underside white with small black spots. Nocturnal, largely aquatic, ovo-viviparous and feeds on fish and frogs. Mildly venomous. Occurs in freshwater, in ditches, streams and ponds. In Singapore, common in inland water bodies in rural areas and forest. Distributed in Southeast Asia from Indochina to western Indonesia.

**Two individuals eating tilapia.**

# WHITE-SPOTTED SLUG SNAKE
## *Pareas margaritophorus*

Squamata: Pareatidae. To 47 cm TL. Unlike other snakes, the scales on its chin are arranged such that they do not leave a median groove. Head distinct from thick-set body. Grey or brown above with a series of white and black spots together on single scales, neck with a broad reddish collar bar. Underside whitish with black spots. Scales smooth. Largely terrestrial but occasionally climbs over vegetation, this nocturnal snake eats land snails and slugs, and is oviparous. Apparently non-venomous. Believed to be introduced in Singapore, the first record was in 2000. Has been found in open scrubland in Mandai, Khatib Bongsu, Lim Chu Kang and Sungei Buloh. Native to southern China through Indochina to the Malay Peninsula (mostly in the north).

Tay Soon Lian

# BLUE-NECKED KEELBACK
*Macropisthodon rhodomelas*

Squamata: Natricidae. To 52 cm TL. Head distinct from stout body, dorsal scales keeled. Above orange-brown with a black chevron mark over the back of the neck of which the apex points backwards and continues as a black mid-dorsal stripe down to the tail. The sides of the neck are powder blue, and posterior to that is a series of narrow oblique blackish bands along the sides. Underside pink with small black spots. Found in forest, but also in plantations and gardens. This diurnal and terrestrial species feeds largely on frogs. It is known to be **venomous**. When provoked, it flattens its neck like a cobra, and even plays dead. In Singapore, recorded mainly from the Central Nature Reserves. Distributed in the Malay Peninsula, Sumatra, Borneo and Java.

Benjamin Y. H. Lee

# PAINTED MOCK VIPER
*Psammodynastes pictus*

Squamata: Natricidae. To 52 cm TL. Head rather flat, body orange or light brown above with a dark brown vertebral stripe and pairs of yellow spots that may form a chequered pattern; underside yellow with black dots. Found in swamp-forest, along streams where it seems to be primarily arboreal. It is mildly venomous, and is known to feed on fish and shrimps. In Singapore, only from the Central Catchment Nature Reserve. The species occurs in Peninsular Malaysia, Borneo and Sumatra.

# SPOTTED KEELBACK
## *Xenochrophis maculatus*

Squamata: Natricidae. To 81 cm TL. Head distinct from body, dorsal scales strongly keeled. Eye large, as wide as the snout is long, and about twice the depth of the upper lip. Dark brown or grey above with squarish black blotches on the neck. Along the back, a broad dark brown stripe with black blotches within, and yellow squarish blotches at regular intervals along the outer margins. Reddish on the sides. Underside yellow with black edged ventral scales. Upper lip yellow or white with narrow black bands. Inhabits forest and is terrestrial and diurnal in habits. It feeds on frogs, and is apparently non-venomous. In Singapore, confined to the Central Nature Reserves. Distributed in the Malay Peninsula, Sumatra and Borneo.

Chan Kwok Wai

# STRIPED KEELBACK
## *Xenochrophis vittatus*

Squamata: Natricidae. To 70 cm TL. Head distinct from body, dorsal scales strongly keeled. Black above with four yellowish brown stripes from neck to tail. Upper lip white with broad black bands. Underside white, each ventral scale with a broad black band. In-habits open fields and scrubland where this terrestrial species is diurnal. It feeds mainly on frogs and small fish, and appears to be non-venomous. Most likely introduced in Singapore where it was first reported in the mid-1980's. Presently common in the Lim Chu Kang, Neo Tiew and Jurong areas, in rural and suburban habitats. Native to Sumatra, Java and Sulawesi.

Nick Baker

# BANDED KRAIT
*Bungarus fasciatus*

Squamata: Elapidae. To 1.5 m TL. Head slightly distinct from body. Body thick-set, some-what triangular in cross-section, scales smooth. White or yellowish above with a series of black bars which extend onto the belly, and are as broad as the pale-coloured segments. Head mostly black with blunt snout, tip of tail blunt. Inhabits forest, scrubland and mangroves where it is mainly terrestrial and nocturnal, and feeds chiefly on other snakes and lizards. A highly **venomous** snake whose bite can be fatal to humans. In Singapore, it is recently recorded from seashore habitats at Pulau Ubin, Pulau Tekong, Lim Chu Kang, Sungei Buloh and Khatib Bongsu. Widely distributed in Southeast Asia.

Ria Tan

# BLUE MALAYAN CORAL SNAKE
*Calliophis bivirgatus* (formerly as *Maticora bivirgata*)

Squamata: Elapidae. To 1.8 m TL. Head small and slightly distinct from very slender body. Dark navy blue on the back, a powder blue stripe along the sides, coral red on the underside. Head and tail bright coral red. This strikingly coloured snake inhabits mainly forest, where it is both terrestrial and semi-fossorial, and feeds on other snakes. Although

presumed to have nocturnal habits, individuals are often observed in the early morning on forest trails. When cornered, it has been observed to coil up and wiggle its raised red tail. Highly **venomous**. In Singapore, it is found in the Central Nature Reserves and the Western Catchment Area. Distributed in the Malay Peninsula, Sumatra, Borneo and Java.

# BANDED MALAYAN CORAL SNAKE
## *Calliophis intestinalis* (formerly as *Maticora intestinalis*)

Squamata: Elapidae. To 71 cm TL. Head small and barely distinct from very slender body. Dark brown above with a red mid-dorsal stripe. Underside of body white with black bands, underside of tail bright red with black bands. This semi-fossorial and nocturnal species inhabits forest, scrubland and gardens. It feeds on other small snakes, such as the blind snakes. When harassed, it flattens its body, becomes rigid and exposes its banded underside. This species is highly **venomous**, but can be confused with the harmless Striped Kukri Snake. In Singapore, it is found in forest as well as rural and suburban areas. Distributed in the Malay Peninsula, Sumatra, Borneo and Java.

Nick Baker

Nick Baker

**Topside (top) and underside**

# EQUATORIAL SPITTING COBRA or BLACK SPITTING COBRA
## *Naja sumatrana*

Squamata: Elapidae. To 1 m TL. Head broad and slightly distinct from body. Body stout and cylindrical in cross-section, with stretchable fold of skin on both sides of the neck. Uniform iridescent black above. Underside bluish-grey with white blotches on the throat and neck. Mainly diurnal and terrestrial in habits, it feeds on small animals such as rats and toads, and occurs in forest, scrubland and gardens. This highly **venomous** snake will raise the front part of its body when provoked, flatten its neck and hiss loudly. If this warning display fails, it may eject fine sprays of venom from its fangs towards the eyes of its provoker. The spray can cover a distance of over one metre, and can cause considerable discomfort and even temporary blindness if it enters the eyes. Therefore do not approach a cobra, especially an irate one, too closely. In Singapore, this snake is common in scrubland and suburban areas, and individuals sometimes enter houses. Distributed in the Malay Peninsula, Sumatra and Borneo.

Nick Baker

**In defensive posture**

Nick Baker

# KING COBRA
## *Ophiophagus hannah*

Squamata: Elapidae. To 5.8 m TL. Body long but stout, head broad with stretchable fold of skin on both sides of neck. Adults brown or olive above with dark-edged scales; throat orange with dark markings; underside greyish. Juveniles black above with narrow yellow or white bands. This mainly terrestrial and diurnal snake occurs in forest and scrubland. Other snakes and monitor lizards form the bulk of its natural diet. The female lays her eggs in a specially constructed nest of vegetation and guards these until they hatch. It is highly **venomous** and dangerous. Recorded from the Central Nature Reserves, Sungei Buloh area, Kranji, the Western Catchment Area, Sentosa and Pulau Tekong. The species is widespread from India to southern China and throughout Southeast Asia.

**Adult (top) and juvenile form**

# AMPHIBIOUS SEA SNAKE or YELLOW-LIPPED SEA KRAIT
*Laticauda colubrina*

Squamata: Hydrophiidae. To 1.4 m TL. Head slightly distinct from the slender body which ends in a flattened, paddle-shaped tail. Bluish-grey with black bands; head marked with black and yellow. Mainly aquatic in habits, but unlike other sea snakes (that are helpless on land), it readily comes ashore to rest and lay eggs. It inhabits coral reefs and rocky shorelines; and feeds on fish, especially eels. This **venomous** snake is reputed to have a docile disposition. In Singapore, it is known only from the Southern Islands and other surrounding coral reefs. It has a wide distribution in the Indo-west Pacific.

# MANGROVE PIT-VIPER or SHORE PIT-VIPER
*Cryptelytrops purpureomaculatus* (formerly as *Trimeresurus purpureomaculatus*)

Squamata: Viperidae. To 1 m TL. Head broadly triangular from top view, very distinct from relatively stout body which is covered in keeled scales. Uniform purplish-brown with a narrow white stripe along each side of the ventrum. Hatchlings have dark brown saddle bars along the back. This arboreal, live-bearing species feeds on lizards and perhaps small birds. It inhabits mangroves and forest along the coast. By day this nocturnally active snake lies quietly coiled amongst mangrove vegetation. **Venomous** and aggressive. When threat-

ened, it has been observed to shake its tail vigorously against vegetation, making a rattling sound reminiscent of a rattlesnake. In Singapore, it is recorded from Sungei Buloh Wetland Reserve, Lim Chu Kang, Sentosa Island, Pasir Ris and Pulau Ubin. Distributed along the coasts of the Malay Peninsula and Sumatra.

# WAGLER'S PIT-VIPER
*Tropidolaemus wagleri*

Squamata: Viperidae. To 98 cm TL. Head broadly triangular from top view, very distinct from relatively stout body which is covered in keeled scales. Adult females black above with green spots and yellow bands, underside greenish white with yellow patches. Juveniles and the considerably smaller-sized males are green with pairs of short red and white bars along the back, a red and white stripe along the sides of the head, and a red tail. Nocturnal and arboreal, often encountered on low shrubs where it tends to be sluggish during the day. Live-bearing and feeds on small vertebrates. This **venomous** species mainly inhabits mature forest. In Singapore, apparently restricted to the Central Nature Reserves and Pulau Tekong.

Leong Tzi Ming

**Adult female (above) and male**

Chan Kwok Wai

Bukit Timah Oct. '09 ♂ or juv. ☐ ♀

# ESTUARINE CROCODILE or SALTWATER CROCODILE
## *Crocodylus porosus*

Crocodylia: Crocodylidae. Reported to attain 9 m TL, but usually much smaller. Snout long and relatively broad, tail muscular and compressed; body yellow, olive or grey above with black checker-spots, and white below. In Singapore, has been recorded in estuaries and reservoirs. This amphibious creature spends most of the day basking at the water's edge or concealed among vegetation. It hunts mainly at night in the water for fish and other small animals. This species attains breeding size at around 3 m TL. The eggs are laid in a specially constructed nest of vegetation, and are savagely guarded by the female. In Singapore, crocodiles have been reported (and captured) from the estuaries of the Singapore and Kallang rivers, and the Sungei Seletar and Kranji Reservoirs. They have also been observed in mangrove and prawn pond areas at Sungei Buloh Wetland Reserve and Pulau Tekong. The species is widespread throughout the Indo West Pacific. Although internationally acknowledged as an endangered species, successful captive breeding in farms, especially in Southeast Asia and Australia, has reduced hunting pressure on wild populations.

# MALAYAN BOX TERRAPIN
## *Cuora amboinensis*

Testudines: Geoemydidae. To 25 cm CL. Carapace highly domed in side profile, uniformly black, with five vertebral scutes and smooth margins. Plastron yellowish with a hinge across the middle that enable both ends of the plastron to be lifted upwards and seal the turtle completely inside its shell. Head black above with a bright stripe on both sides. Semi-aquatic to terrestrial in habits, it is omnivorous (more herbivorous) and frequents streams, ponds and reservoirs in forest and rural areas. In Singapore, common along the edges of the reservoirs in the Central Catchment Nature Reserve. It is also found in the Botanic Gardens and on Pulau Ubin. It is possible that a large part of the local population consists of released individuals. Distributed in northeast India and throughout Southeast Asia.

Nick Baker

# ASIAN LEAF TERRAPIN
## *Cyclemys dentata*

Testudines: Geoemydidae. To 24 cm CL. Sides of carapace convex when viewed from the top. Carapace blackish brown with five vertebral scutes, posterior margin serrated. Plastral scutes with blackish radiating lines. Head and neck dark brown with orange lines. Hatchlings have a relatively flat carapace that is greyish brown covered in dense black spots. Inhabits forest streams where it is semi-aquatic and omnivorous in habits. In Singapore, known from the Western Catchment Area. Widely distributed in Southeast Asia.

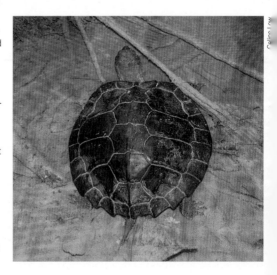

Celine Low

# SPINY TERRAPIN or SPINY HILL TERRAPIN
## *Heosemys spinosa*

Testudines: Geoemydidae. To 23 cm CL. Carapace with a flat top in side view, brown with serrated rear margin and a pale brown mid-dorsal ridge, and five vertebral scutes. Plastral scutes with blackish radiating lines. Head and limbs dark grey; a reddish spot on each side of the head. The carapace of hatchlings appears more flat and heart-shaped in top view, the margins with spiky serrations. Inhabits mature forest where it seems to be nocturnally active and omnivorous. Adults are terrestrial in habits, while juveniles are more amphibious. In Singapore, native populations of this species are confined to the Central Nature Reserves. Distributed in the Malay Peninsula, Sumatra, Borneo and Mindanao.

**Juvenile (left) and adult**

## MALAYAN FLATSHELL TERRAPIN
*Notochelys platynota*

Testudines: Geoemydidae. To 37 cm CL. Carapace brown with a distinctly flat top and a sharply sloping posterior profile in side view, rear margin serrated, no mid-dorsal ridge. Distinguished from all local turtles in having six, or even seven, vertebral scutes (instead of five). Head brown with or without reddish stripes, limbs brown. The carapace of hatchlings are bright green with small black spots. This semi-aquatic, omnivorous (largely frugivorous) turtle inhabits forest streams. In Singapore, it is recorded from the Central Catchment Nature Reserve and the Western Catchment Area. Distributed in continental Southeast Asia, as well as on Sumatra, Borneo and Java.

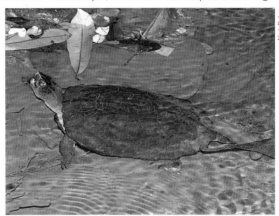
Nick Baker

## BLACK MARSH TERRAPIN
*Siebenrockiella crassicollis*

Testudines: Geoemydidae. To 20 cm CL. Sides of carapace straight when viewed from the top. Carapace black, domed in side view and serrated along the rear margin, with five vertebral scutes. Plastron black with brown streaks. Head black with white spots, limbs black. Largely aquatic and carnivorous, and seems to be active both day and night. Found in streams, ponds and reservoirs in forest and rural areas. This is one of the species frequently released as religious merit-making offerings, and may not be native to Singapore. Distributed in continental Southeast Asia, Sumatra, Borneo and Java.

Chan Kwok Wai

# RED-EARED SLIDER or ELEGANT SLIDER
## *Trachemys scripta elegans*

Testudines: Emydidae. To 28 cm CL. Carapace olive brown with yellowish streaks, domed in side view, with five vertebral scutes, and without serrated margins. Plastron yellow with a round black spot on each scute. Head green with numerous yellow stripes and a broad bright red streak behind the eye. Limbs and tail green with yellow stripes. Mature males have long claws on their forelimbs and use these to 'tickle' female partners on their heads during courtship rituals. Found in ponds and reservoirs. This diurnal and omnivorous turtle is largely aquatic. In Singapore, it is a common feral species. Most individuals being abandoned pets or religious merit-making offerings. Native to North America.

Nick Baker

Chan Kwok Wai

**Adult and head of hatchling (inset)** S.B.Gs all years

Kelvin Lim

The **Cuban Slider** (*Trachemys decussatus*) from Central America (left) is a closely related species that is sometimes seen in the feral state in Singapore. It is distinguished from the Red-eared Slider in lacking stripes and red blotches on the head.

## ASIAN SOFTSHELL TURTLE
*Amyda cartilaginea*

Testudines: Trionychidae. To over 75 cm CL. Carapace roughly squarish, leathery without scutes, but with numerous short ridges on the surface. Carapace greyish brown with irregular blackish bands. Numerous yellow spots on the head and limbs, and sometimes the carapace. Underside white. Snout proboscis-like, neck long, feet clawed and fully-webbed. Aquatic, inhabits shallow forest streams with a soft sand substrate. It is nocturnal,

and spends the day buried in the substrate and ambushes passing fish, frogs, crustaceans and insects. It also eats fruits and seeds. In Singapore, known largely from the Central Catchment Nature Reserve. Distributed throughout Southeast Asia except in the Philippines.

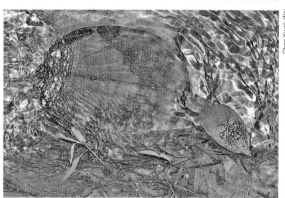

Chan Kwok Wai

## CHINESE SOFTSHELL TURTLE
*Pelodiscus sinensis*

Testudines: Trionychidae. To 35 cm CL. Carapace smooth and leathery without scutes, oval-shaped, with a ridge at the front edge. Snout proboscis-like, neck long, feet clawed and fully-webbed. Greyish brown above uniform or with numerous yellow and blackish spots. Head with fine black streaks radiating from the eye, side of neck with a whitish stripe. Underside whitish on adults, orange on hatchlings. Inhabits freshwater where it spends the day buried in the substrate to ambush

Chan Kwok Wai

small animals. In Singapore, this species is bred commercially for food, and individuals are often released in ponds and reservoirs as religious merit making offerings. It is not known if this feral population is self-perpetuating. Native to temperate China and Japan.

# MALAYAN FOREST SOFTSHELL TURTLE
## *Dogania subplana*

Testudines: Trionychidae. To 35 cm CL. Carapace smooth and leathery without scutes, oval-shaped, yellowish-brown with a black mid-dorsal stripe and often with two black ocelli on either side of the stripe. Underside white. Snout proboscis-like, neck long and reddish, feet clawed and fully webbed. Aquatic, inhabits shaded shallow streams with fast-flowing water, and a soft sand substrate, in mature forest. It is nocturnal, and spends the day buried in the substrate and ambushes passing fish, frogs and insects. It also eats mollusks and crustaceans. In Singapore, known only from the Central Catchment Nature Reserve. It occurs in Thailand, Peninsular Malaysia, Sumatra, Borneo and Java.

Nick Baker

**Juvenile (left) and adult**

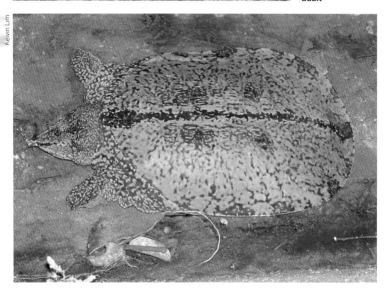

Kelvin Lim

**Sunda Slow Loris
(*Nycticebus coucang*)**
Chan Kwok Wai

# MAMMALS

The first mammals appeared in the Jurassic and Cretaceous periods, when they co-existed with dinosaurs. Around 65 million years ago, after the extinction of the dinosaurs, mammals diversified into a wide range of species with different body forms and modes of life. Many became larger to fill ecological niches left vacant by the dinosaurs.

Mammals range in size from the tiniest bat to the largest creature on earth, the Blue Whale. They are dispersed throughout the globe in a huge variety of habitats from deserts to rainforests, and from polar regions to the deep oceans. In tropical forests they can climb to the canopy (e.g. monkeys), glide from tree to tree (e.g. colugos), fly in the sky (e.g. bats), or burrow in the soil (e.g. porcupines).

They exhibit a high degree of parental care. In placental mammals, the unborn young develop inside the womb to a considerable size whilst attached to the placenta. Once born the young are suckled on milk produced by the mammary glands of the female and, even after being weaned, are cared for until adulthood. Milk production, or lactation, is one of the key identifying features of mammals.

Mammals are endothermic or "warm-blooded", meaning they are able to control their body temperature to within a narrow range. This adaptation allows them to be active when ambient temperatures are cooler than normal and other "cold-blooded" animals, such as reptiles or amphibians, become largely inactive. Birds are also warm-blooded.

Most mammals are covered with fur or hair, which plays a role in conserving body heat, though in some species this may be sparse. The pangolin has hair that is compacted into large, overlapping scales to help protect it from being bitten by ants, its main food source.

Perhaps the most successful of modern mammal groups are **RODENTS** (order Rodentia).

Rodents have enlarged incisor teeth, which are ever-growing and used for gnawing. Squirrels (family Sciuridae) have long bushy tails, and many species are arboreal. They can be divided into two groups: those with gliding membranes (flying squirrels) are nocturnal, and those without (tree and ground squirrels) tend to be diurnal.

Singapore's most conspicuous mammal, the ubiquitous Plantain Squirrel, is found in many terrestrial habitats. The country's rarest mammal is, arguably, the Cream-coloured Giant Squirrel (*Ratufa affinis*). See photo on page 6. First described from Singapore by Sir Stamford Raffles in 1821, this magnificent rodent, measuring up to 80 cm in total length, has not been seen locally since 1995 and, to our knowledge, there are no photographs taken locally of the species in its natural habitat.

Rats (family Muridae) are easily distinguished by their long pointed muzzles, and long tails that are usually covered with short, fine hairs. In some species, the upper body fur is mixed with spines, and in porcupines (family Hystricidae) much of the fur is modified into long, stiff spines which offer effective protection against predators.

**SHREWS** (order Soricomorpha, family Soricidae) resemble

mice in appearance, but differ in having a longer snout, small beady eyes, and a row of pointed teeth along the jaws. They also tend to have short and very dense fur that somewhat resembles velvet. Shrews are largely insectivorous.

**TREESHREWS** (order Scandentia) strongly

resemble squirrels in having large eyes and bushy tails. They are distinguished from the latter by having a long, pointed snout, and, like shrews, a row of pointed teeth along the jaws. Treeshrews forage mainly on the forest floor for insects and fruit. They are partly arboreal, but tend to climb no higher than one or two metres from the ground.

**BATS** form the order Chiroptera, and are the only mammals capable of true flight. Their wings comprise a leathery  membrane stretched over the arms, hands and long, slender fingers, and connected to the sides of the body, the legs and feet. Morphologically, bats can be divided into two major groups:

The suborder Megachiroptera includes bats with large eyes, long muzzles and dog-like faces. They have excellent night vision, and a few species are also known to use echolocation to navigate. They feed on fruit and nectar, and play important roles in dispersing seeds and pollinating flowers, especially those of fruit trees such as the durian. Members of the family Pteropodidae are known as "fruit bats" and the larger members as "flying foxes". The Common Fruit Bat can easily be observed in all parts of Singapore, especially when figs are fruiting.

The suborder Microchiroptera includes bats with small eyes and generally short muzzles. All microchiropterans have excellent hearing, and are experts at using high frequency echolocation to navigate and locate prey in darkness. In the families Rhinolophidae and Hipposideridae, the muzzle is covered with complex arrangements of skin folds (nose-leaves), which play a role in echolocation. These structures are also present in the families Megadermatidae and Nycteridae, but are less complex, and are absent in the Emballonuridae, Molossidae and Vespertilionidae. Most species in this group feed on flying insects, and some may be seen at dusk in urban areas catching insects attracted to street lights.

**COLUGOS** (order Dermoptera) are an ancient group of mammals which have a membrane of skin extending all  around the body, stretching to the tips of its long limbs and tail. This feature enables the animal to glide from tree to tree. This nocturnally active herbivore lives in primary and secondary forest.

**PANGOLINS** (order Pholidota) are instantly recognised by their scale-cov-  ered body. These scales are actually modified hair. Pangolins have short limbs, large claws, a prehensile tail and an extremely long, flexible, sticky tongue with which ants and termites are drawn into the mouth.

**CARNIVORES** (order Carnivora) have the fourth upper premolar and the first lower molar  modified into two long pointed teeth that slide against each other like scissor blades. The word carnivore means "flesh-eater", and these sharp, canine teeth have evolved to effectively rip and tear flesh. However, many species in this group are omnivorous, and a few (e.g. the Giant Panda) are even herbivorous.

Cats (family Felidae) have relatively flat faces, short erect ears, and are almost exclusively carnivorous. The Leopard Cat is the sole surviving example in modern Singapore. The Tiger (*Panthera tigris*), the largest member of the cat family, once existed in Singapore but, because of its occasional taste for human flesh, was widely persecuted. The last local specimen was shot in Choa Chu Kang village in the 1930s. Civets (family Viverridae) have long muzzles, long bodies, long tails and short limbs, and most have a special scent gland, known as the civet gland, located in their genital region. Civets are usually omnivorous, feeding mainly on fruits, but sometimes stealing bird eggs or chicks from vulnerable nests. Some species are arboreal while others live mainly on the ground. The Common Palm Civet still thrives in leafy, urban areas where there is sufficient food and places to nest, such as tree holes or roof spaces.

The family Mustelidae is represented in Singapore by two species of otter. Otters are characterised by their small ears, long bodies, webbed feet, and aquatic habits. An encounter with these gregarious and highly vocal animals is always a special moment. Fish and crustaceans appear to form a large part of their diet.

### EVEN-TOED HOOFED

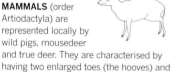

**MAMMALS** (order Artiodactyla) are represented locally by wild pigs, mousedeer and true deer. They are characterised by having two enlarged toes (the hooves) and slender legs.

Pigs (family Suidae) have compact bodies and large heads with small eyes and a tubular snout. They are omnivores that use their snout and long upper canine teeth or tusks to root in the soil to turn up tubers and worms. The Wild Pig is Singapore's largest resident mammal.

Mousedeer (family Tragulidae) are small, rabbit-sized relatives of true deer. They have large eyes and very skinny, relatively short legs. Males do not have antlers, but the canine teeth in the upper jaws are long and protrude out of the mouth. The diminutive Lesser Mousedeer still survives in the Central Nature Reserves. Two species of true deer (family Cervidae) once roamed Singapore, but became extinct before the Second World War.

### PRIMATES (order Primates)

have rounded heads with forward facing eyes, short muzzles and long grasping digits with nails instead of claws. The arboreal and solitary slow loris (family Lorisidae) resembles a teddy bear with its brown fur, large rounded eyes, and short tail. It is active at night and feeds on insects and fruit. Monkeys (family Cercopithecidae) are active in the day and are highly gregarious. The rare Banded Leaf Monkey is herbivorous and keeps to the trees, while the common Long-tailed Macaque is omnivorous, often foraging for food on the ground.

Let us not forget that human beings (*Homo sapiens*) are also primates. They are locally very abundant and have the capability to exploit and change the environment to suit their needs. As a result, they cause massive damage to natural habitats, and have forced many wildlife species into extinction.

It is hard to imagine Southeast Asia's largest land mammal, the Asian Elephant (*Elephas maximus*, family Elephantidae, order Proboscidea), roaming Singapore. The island state is simply too small to support a resident population of these giant beasts. However, in 1990 three bull elephants landed on Pulau Tekong, having swum across the Johor Straits from Malaysia, and the next year another made it to Pulau Ubin. Despite their size, elephants are in fact excellent swimmers. Their long, mobile trunks can be held above water allowing them to keep breathing even in choppy seas. These were the first local records ever for these magnificent creatures, but their stay was short-lived. They were soon rounded up with the assistance of the Malaysian Wildlife Department and returned up-country to more suitable habitat.

Apart from the Wild Pig, most large mammals lack sufficient space to maintain viable populations in Singapore. However, there remains a fairly diverse mammal fauna here. Among these, some medium-sized species such as the Banded Leaf Monkey, Sunda Slow Loris and Leopard Cat are at risk of local extinction. It is hoped that our remaining forests, under careful management, are able to regenerate in time for populations of these key species to be pulled back from the brink.

# COMMON TREESHREW
*Tupaia glis*

Scandentia: Tupaiidae. HB to 20.5 cm, T to 19.5 cm. Muzzle long and tapering, jaws with pointed teeth, limbs short, tail long and bushy. Shoulders and torso reddish-brown above; dark greyish brown on tail, limbs and top of head; yellowish below. Yellowish ring around eye, and usually a whitish oblique stripe over the shoulders. Occurs mainly in forest and adjacent scrubland and parkland where it is diurnal and forages alone or in pairs, mainly on the ground and among shrubs, for insects and fruit. In Singapore, it occurs in the Central Nature Reserves, the Western Catchment Area, Bukit Batok Nature Park, Botanic Gardens and Kent Ridge. Distributed in the Malay Peninsula and Sumatra.

Nick Baker

Bukit Timah    '08, '09 ; MacRitchie Res.    '08 ; SBG 0

# MALAYAN COLUGO or MALAYAN FLYING LEMUR
*Galeopterus variegatus* (formerly as *Cynocephalus variegatus*)

Dermoptera: Cynocephalidae. HB to 38 cm, T to 26.5 cm. Muzzle pointed, eyes very large, limbs long, feet with large claws. Extensive skin membrane stretching from neck to forelimbs, between the digits, along the side of the body, the hind limbs and across the long tail. Either grey or reddish-brown above, mostly with irregular narrow black bands and streaks, and white blotches, and a whitish eye ring. Solitary, arboreal and nocturnal in habit, usually spends the day clinging to tree trunks, or suspended from horizontal branches. Feeds largely on leaves. Infant clings to the underside of its mother's torso. Able to glide long distances between trees. In Singapore, it occurs mainly in the Central Nature Reserves and adjacent plantations and parkland, and in Bukit Batok Nature Park. Distributed in Myanmar, Indochina, the Malay Peninsula, Sumatra, Borneo and Java.

Norman Lim

Kid Lim

**Female with young and gliding individual (inset)**

Bukit Timah near Hindhede quarry 2007, '09

MAMMALS

## SUNDA SLOW LORIS
*Nycticebus coucang*

Norman Lim

Primates: Lorisidae. HB to 30 cm, T to 3 cm. Head round with very short muzzle and large, forward-facing eyes. Body stocky with soft and dense fur, relatively slender limbs and very short tail. Pale greyish to reddish brown with a brown mid-dorsal stripe, and usually a dark coloured ring around each eye. Inhabits forest. Nocturnal, arboreal and usually solitary. Its movements may appear deliberate, but not necessarily slow. Frugivorous and carnivorous. One of a few mammals whose bite is known to be venomous. Due to their attractive appearance, individuals are often caught and sold as pets. In Singapore, recorded from the Central Nature Reserves, and from Pulau Tekong. Distributed in the Malay Peninsula, Sumatra and adjacent islands.

## LONG-TAILED MACAQUE or CRAB-EATING MACAQUE
*Macaca fascicularis*

Primates: Cercopithecidae. HB 45.5 cm, T to 56.5 cm. Head round with forward-directing eyes, muzzle very short. Limbs and tail long, hairs on head lie flat. Olive brown above, paler below, greyish on the face with prominent white eyelids. Diurnal, omnivorous and mainly arboreal, although also forages on the ground. Its call sounds like "krraaa". Gregarious, usually lives in a troop of about 30 individuals comprising two to four adult males and six to eleven adult females and their offspring. Frequents forest and adjacent parkland. In Singapore, it occurs in the Central Nature Reserves, the Western Catchment Area, Bukit Batok Nature Park, Sentosa, the Sisters' Islands, Sungei Buloh Wetland Reserve, Pulau Ubin and Pulau Tekong.

Nick Baker

Tan Heok Hui

Male (left) and females with infant

*Bukit Timah — all years*
*Mac Ritchie — all years*
*SBG '09*

# BANDED LEAF MONKEY, BANDED LANGUR or RAFFLES'S SURILI
*Presbytis femoralis* (formerly confused with *Presbytis melalophos*)

Primates: Cercopithecidae. HB to 59 cm, T to 84 cm. Head round with forward-directing eyes, muzzle very short. Limbs and tail long, abdomen protruding, hair on head directed towards the centre of the crown where they stand erect. Adults black with a white line down the middle of the chest and belly. Inner parts of arms and legs to just below the knee are white. Prominent white eye ring and a whitish crescent-shaped mark on each side of face between the eye and the ear. Infants are white to pale grey, although orange-coloured* infants have been reported. Inhabits mature forest where it is active in the day. Arboreal and gregarious, its diet consists principally of fruit and new leaves. Its alarm call resembles the rattle of a machine gun. This species was first described from Singapore in 1838. In Singapore, it appears that only around 20 individuals are left and presently restricted to the Central Catchment Nature Reserve. Distributed in the Malay Peninsula and eastern Sumatra.

Daniel Koh

* This is unusual for the genus *Presbytis*, for their infants are supposed to be white. Orange-coloured infants are characteristic of leaf monkeys in the genus *Trachypithecus*, such as the Silvered Leaf Monkey and the Dusky Leaf Monkey, both of which are common in Peninsular Malaysia, but not known to occur naturally in Singapore.

Daniel Koh

RODENTS

## VARIABLE SQUIRREL
### *Callosciurus finlaysonii*

Rodentia: Sciuridae. HB to 21 cm, T to 24 cm. Head round, snout blunt, with short legs and a long bushy tail. Colour variable – black, grey or dark brown above and on the tail, sharply contrasted with cream on the underside; or entirely cream from head to tail. May also be uniformly red or black, or grey-and-red. Diurnal, omnivorous and frequents trees. Introduced in Singapore probably since the early 1990's. Feral population mainly in the Aljunied area, in suburban parkland and cemeteries. Native to Thailand where it is the common urban squirrel in Bangkok.

Chan Kwok Wai

# PLANTAIN SQUIRREL or RED-BELLIED SQUIRREL
*Callosciurus notatus*

Rodentia: Sciuridae. HB to 22 cm, T to 21 cm. Head round, snout blunt, with short legs and a long bushy tail. Olive-brown above and on the tail, belly and inside of limbs reddish-brown, a black and white stripe on each side of the body and whitish around the eyes. Diurnal, omnivorous and arboreal. Inhabits forest, mangrove, scrubland and parkland. Builds a spherical nest of twigs. In Singapore, widespread and common, even in housing estates. Distributed in the Malay Peninsula, Sumatra, Borneo and Java.

SBG

# SLENDER SQUIRREL
*Sundasciurus tenuis*

Rodentia: Sciuridae. HB to 15 cm, T to 13 cm. Head round, snout blunt, with short legs and a furry tail. Upperparts of body and tail olive brown, underside of body grey, pale around the eyes. Tail slender, slightly shorter or slightly longer than HB. Diurnal, omnivorous and arboreal. Inhabits forest and parkland. In Singapore, common but confined to the Central Nature Reserves, Bukit Batok Nature Park and the Botanic Gardens. Distributed in the Malay Peninsula, Sumatra and Borneo.

Bukit Timah
SBG

# RED-CHEEKED FLYING SQUIRREL
## *Hylopetes spadiceus*

Rodentia: Sciuridae. HB to 18.4 cm, T to 16.6 cm. Head round, snout blunt, tail long and feather-like. Large flap of skin with thin white margin present between the limbs on each side of the body. Upperparts dark greyish-brown with rust-coloured markings, underparts white with orange tinge. Base of tail orange, cheeks orange-brown on grey. This tiny, nocturnal squirrel lives in primary forest, and nests in small holes on the trunk of tall trees. Locally known only from Bukit Timah Nature Reserve where the first local sightings were made in 1996. Distributed in Myanmar, Indochina, the Malay Peninsula, Sumatra and Borneo.

Robert Teo

# HORSFIELD'S FLYING SQUIRREL
## *Iomys horsfieldii*

Rodentia: Sciuridae. HB to 23 cm, T to 20.7 cm. Head round, snout blunt, tail long and feather-like. Large flap of skin fringed with rusty brown present between the limbs on each side of the body. Upperparts dark brown, orange-buff or whitish below, feather-like tail reddish brown. Upper surface of ear lobe virtually hairless. Occurs in primary and secondary forest, and orchards. Nocturnal and arboreal, feeds on fruit and insects. In Singapore, found in the Central Nature Reserves. Distributed in the Malay Peninsula, Sumatra, Borneo and Java.

Normal Lim

Alan Yeo

# BROWN SPINY RAT or RAJAH SPINY RAT
## *Maxomys rajah*

Rodentia: Muridae. HB to 23.5 cm, T to 21 cm (but may be longer than HB). Snout pointed, with short limbs and a long almost naked tail. Upperparts dull brown, sometimes tinged with red or orange; underparts white, with a dark brown streak along the middle in adults, and never with a chestnut collar at base of neck. Coat with numerous stiff spines. Tail brown above, whitish below. Inhabits mature forest. Nocturnal and largely terrestrial. Feeds on fallen fruits, shoots and insects. In Singapore, known from the Central Catchment Nature Reserve, and first reported in 1995. Distributed in the Malay Peninsula, Sumatra, Borneo and Java.

Alan Yeo

Norman Lim

# HOUSE MOUSE
## *Mus musculus*

Rodentia: Muridae. HB to 9 cm, T longer than HB. Snout pointed, with short limbs and a long almost naked tail. Upperparts greyish brown, underparts slightly paler. Ears large, coat with soft fur and no spines. Tail uniformly dark brown. Inhabits buildings where it is nocturnal and omnivorous. Found throughout Singapore, but more commonly in rural areas such as Pulau Ubin. Widespread in India, China and Southeast Asia.

## ANNANDALE'S RAT
## or SINGAPORE RAT
### *Rattus annandalei*

Rodentia: Muridae. HB to 22 cm, T to 27 cm. Snout pointed, with short limbs and a long almost naked tail. Upperparts greyish-brown, fur soft and shaggy without prominent spines. Underparts yellowish white. Tail uniformly brown. Omnivorous and nocturnal, climbs trees with ease. Occurs in secondary forest and scrubland in Singapore. Distributed in the Malay Peninsula and Sumatra.

Benjamin Y.H. Lee

## HOUSE RAT
### *Rattus rattus*

Rodentia: Muridae. HB to 22 cm, T to 22 cm (but can be longer than HB). Snout pointed, with short limbs and a long almost naked tail. Upperparts finely grizzled olive brown, underparts slightly paler. Tail uniformly brown. Omnivorous, nocturnal, and largely solitary, it lives in and around houses. An excellent climber which often frequents roof spaces in buildings. In Singapore, common in low buildings, in gardens and in scrubland. Widespread in East Asia and Southeast Asia. Pending a detailed study, some, if not all, of Singapore's house rats may be referred to as the Tanezumi Rat (*Rattus tanezumi*), which is very similar in appearance but is genetically a different species.

Tsang Kwok Choong

# BROWN RAT
## *Rattus norvegicus*

Rodentia: Muridae. HB to 26.5 cm, T to 23 cm (always shorter than HB). Snout pointed, with short limbs and a long almost naked tail. Upperparts brown, hair coarse but without prominent spines. Underparts greyish brown or grey. Tail may be entirely brown or slightly pale below. Omnivore that lives mainly at ground level and shelters in burrows. Mainly active at night, but can also be seen in the day outside its burrow. In Singapore, common in public housing estates. Although it can climb, it appears to restrict its activities to the ground. Distributed throughout the world especially where there are large cities.

Kelvin Lim

# MALAYSIAN WOOD RAT
## *Rattus tiomanicus*

Rodentia: Muridae. HB to 19 cm, T to 19.8 cm (can be distinctly longer than HB). Snout pointed, with short limbs and a long almost naked tail. Upperparts finely grizzled olive brown, a little darker in midline. Underparts greyish white. Fur smooth and sleek with short stiff spines. Tail uniformly dark brown. In Singapore, inhabits secondary forest, scrubland, plantations and mangroves. Omnivorous and nocturnal, able to climb with ease. Distributed in the Malay Peninsula, Sumatra, Borneo and Java.

Nick Baker

# MALAYAN PORCUPINE
## *Hystrix brachyura*

Rodentia: Hystricidae. HB to about 70 cm, T to 13 cm. Snout blunt, body robust with short limbs and a relatively short tail. Hair on upperparts modified into stiff long spines, those on the rear back are longest and are black with white bands. Rest of animal blackish with a whitish band across the chest. Inhabits forest and plantations. Nocturnal, herbivorous and usually terrestrial, but excavates deep burrows where it spends the day. In Singapore, recently recorded only from Pulau Tekong. Records of large porcupines in the Central Catchment Nature Reserve could be zoo escapees, and may not be of the same species.

Norman Lim

# HOUSE SHREW
*Suncus murinus*

Soricomorpha: Soricidae. HB to 15 cm, T to 9.5 cm. Body long and sleek with short legs, a pointed snout and beady eyes. Coat silvery grey. Tail shorter than head and body, sparsely haired and relatively thick. Commensal with humans, this nocturnal and solitary animal is usually found in and around buildings, but also frequents gardens. It emits shrill and loud shrieks when harassed. Although its diet consists of earthworms and insects such as cockroaches, it is omnivorous and will scavenge on discarded human food. Out in the open, the mother shrew leads her brood in a single file, each young firmly latched with its teeth to the hindquarters of the sibling in front, the first baby to their mother. Widespread in Africa and Asia.

Chan Kwok Wai

# COMMON FRUIT BAT or LESSER DOG-FACED FRUIT BAT
## *Cynopterus brachyotis*

Chiroptera: Pteropodidae. FA to 6.5 cm. Head dog-like with long muzzle and large eyes. Tail short and not linked to flight membrane. Claw on second finger. Brown with a reddish (on males) or yellowish (on females) collar. Ears and wing bones with white edges. Two pairs of lower incisor teeth. Nocturnal, feeds on nectar and fruit. Roosts in trees under clumps of bird's nest ferns, under palm fronds and even in buildings. In Singapore, widespread and common, even in urban areas. Distributed in Sri Lanka, Myanmar and South China, Indochina, the Philippines, Malaysia and western Indonesia.

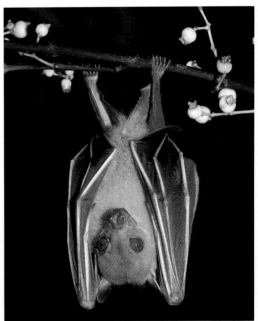

Ria Tan

Chan Kwok Wai

# CAVE NECTAR BAT
*Eonycteris spelaea*

Nick Baker

Chiroptera: Pteropodidae. FA to 7 cm. Head dog-like with large eyes, muzzle long and narrow. Tail short and not linked to flight membrane. No claw on second finger. Dark greyish-brown above, paler below. Roosts in large colonies in caves, old buildings and under concrete bridges. Flies out at dusk to feed on nectar and pollen. In Singapore, widespread but considered rare. Distributed in Myanmar, Indochina, the Philippines, Malaysia and western Indonesia.

# DUSKY FRUIT BAT
*Penthetor lucasi*

Chiroptera: Pteropodidae. FA to 6.2 cm. Head dog-like with long muzzle and large eyes. Tail short and not linked to flight membrane. Claw on second finger. Back dark greyish-brown, pale grey on the underside, ears with dark edges. One pair of lower incisor teeth. Nocturnal frugivore that roosts in caves and under rock shelters. It is known to carry fruit back to its roost to eat. In Singapore, recent records restricted to Bukit Timah Nature Reserve. Distributed in the Malay Peninsula, the Riau Islands and Borneo.

# GLOSSY HORSESHOE BAT or BLYTH'S HORSESHOE BAT
## *Rhinolophus lepidus* (formerly as *Rhinolophus refulgens*)

Nick Baker

Chiroptera: Rhinolophidae. FA to 4.2 cm. Muzzle with elaborate noseleaf consisting of a rounded, horseshoe shaped front section, a raised mid-section (sella) and a more elevated lancet-shaped rear section. Fur woolly, bright orange-brown or grey. Noseleaf and ears greyish. Relatively small size. Nocturnal and insectivorous, it inhabits mature forest and roosts in hollow trees, tunnels and in drain culverts. In Singapore, apparently confined to the Central Nature Reserves where it is common. Widely distributed from Afghanistan through India, southern China, continental Southeast Asia and Sumatra.

# TREFOIL HORSESHOE BAT
## *Rhinolophus trifoliatus*

Chiroptera: Rhinolophidae. FA to 5.2 cm. Muzzle with elaborate noseleaf consisting of a rounded, horse-shoe shaped front section, a raised mid-section (sella) and a more elevated lancet-shaped rear section. Fur long and woolly, pale yellowish-brown to greyish-brown. Noseleaf yellow. Ears and wing membranes yellowish brown with yellow elbows and knees. This nocturnal, insectivorous bat inhabits the under-storey of forests and appears to

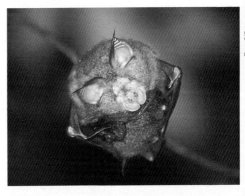

be solitary. It roosts among vegetation, under large leaves. In Singapore, recorded from the Central Catchment Nature Reserve and Pulau Tekong. Distributed in India, Myanmar, Thailand, the Malay Peninsula, Sumatra, Borneo and Java.

# MALAYAN FALSE VAMPIRE or LESSER FALSE VAMPIRE
## *Megaderma spasma*

Norman Lim

Chiroptera: Megadermatidae. FA to 6.1 cm. Muzzle with large, erect noseleaf. Ears large and joined at the base across the top of the head. Fur pale grey to greyish-brown. Nocturnal and inhabits forest. In the day, roosts in small groups in caves, tunnels, hollow trees and old wells. Feeds on insects and other animals, including smaller bats, and does not drink blood. In Singapore, known recently from Pulau Tekong and Pulau Ubin. Distributed in India and Sri Lanka across to Indochina, the Philippines, the Malay Peninsula, Sumatra, Borneo and Java.

# POUCH-BEARING BAT or POUCHED TOMB BAT
## *Saccolaimus saccolaimus* (formerly as *Taphozous saccolaimus*)

Chan Kwok Wai

Chiroptera: Emballonuridae. FA to 7.8 cm. Muzzle short and without noseleaves. Tail short and sticks out from the middle of flight membrane between hind legs. Dorsum blackish brown with white markings, underparts white. Wings distinctly white. Chin naked, adult males with throat pouch. Legs and feet naked. Nocturnal and insectivorous, this bat roosts in colonies (with as many as 300 individuals) within rock crevices, hollow trees, and within buildings. In flight, its echolocating calls can be heard by the human ear. It is widespread and common in Singapore. Distributed in India, Sri Lanka, Indochina through Malaysia and Indonesia to Australia and the Southwest Pacific islands.

## GREY LARGE-FOOTED MYOTIS
*Myotis adversus*

Chiroptera: Vespertilionidae. FA to 4.1 cm. Ears moderately long and triangular, muzzle small and pointed. Feet large with wing membrane attached to ankle. Fur dense and woolly, hair on dorsum dark brown to dark grey with whitish tips, those on ventrum whitish with black bases. Nocturnal, spending the day roosting in drain culverts and in roof spaces of buildings. At dusk, flies low over large water bodies, scooping insects and small fish off the surface with its large feet. In Singapore, widespread and recorded from many locations, including the Central Catchment Nature Reserve and Sungei Buloh. Distributed from the Malay Peninsula, Borneo, Java and Sulawesi through New Guinea to Australia.

Chan Kwok Wai

## WHISKERED MYOTIS
*Myotis muricola*

Chiroptera: Vespertilionidae. FA to 3.8 cm. Ears moderately long and triangular, muzzle small and pointed. Feet small with wing membrane attached to the base of the toes. Hair on dorsum brown to grey with blackish bases, those on ventrum brown to grey with whitish tips. This small nocturnal and insectivorous bat often roosts inside the rolled central leaves of banana plants in rural areas. It is common and widespread in Singapore. Distributed from eastern India, throughout Southeast Asia to New Guinea.

Chan Kwok Wai

# LESSER ASIATIC YELLOW HOUSE BAT
## *Scotophilus kuhlii*

Chiroptera: Vespertilionidae. FA to 5.4 cm. Muzzle broad without noseleaf. Ears with long tragus that curves forward. Body brown above, pale yellowish brown below. One pair of large and conical upper incisor teeth. Its habit of roosting in large colonies (with as many as 400 individuals) in the roof spaces of buildings suggests that it is largely commensal with humans. At dusk, it hawks for insects over wide open spaces. Common and widespread in Singapore. Widely distributed in the Indian subcontinent, southern China and Southeast Asia.

# LESSER BAMBOO BAT and GREATER BAMBOO BAT
## *Tylonycteris pachypus* and *Tylonycteris robustula*

Chiroptera: Vespertilionidae. Body and head dorso-ventrally flattened. Base of thumb and foot with large disk-shaped pads. Both species of bamboo bats are very difficult to distinguish from each other. The Lesser Bamboo Bat (FA to 2.8 cm) is said to have short and fluffy fur, with its back brown to reddish-brown, underparts paler with strong orange tinge. The Greater Bamboo Bat is said to be generally larger (FA to 3.2 cm) and has sleek, dark brown to greyish brown fur on its upperparts. These small, nocturnal, insectivorous bats roost in small groups in the internodes of bamboo (below, left). They enter and exit the roost through small slits made by beetles. Widespread but not common in Singapore. Distributed in India, south China, Indochina, the Philippines, the Malay Peninsula, Sumatra, Borneo and Java, including Bali and Lombok.

# SUNDA PANGOLIN or MALAYAN SCALY ANTEATER
## *Manis javanica*

Pholidota: Manidae. HB to 64.5 cm, T to 56.5 cm. Body robust with short legs; a slender head; and a long, thick, partially prehensile tail. Body and tail covered with rows of hard, overlapping, olive-brown scales. Feet with strong claws. Inhabits forest, scrubland and plantations. Largely nocturnal, diet consists of larvae and adults of termites and ants whose nests are ripped open with its fore-claws, and prey lapped up with its long and sticky tongue. Largely terrestrial, but also climbs trees well, and often shelters in burrows and tree hollows. It curls up into a ball when threatened. The infant rides on its mother's back at the base of her tail. In Singapore, pangolins are found in the Central Nature Reserves, and in rural and scrub areas in Bukit Batok, Western Catchment Area and on the islands of Ubin and Tekong. Distributed in Myanmar and Indochina, through the Malay Peninsula, Borneo, Sumatra and Java, including Bali and Lombok.

Norman Lim

Norman Lim

# LEOPARD CAT
*Prionailurus bengalensis* (formerly as *Felis bengalensis*)

Carnivora: Felidae. HB to 56 cm, T to 26 cm. Head round with very short muzzle and large erect ears with rounded margins. Reddish or yellowish buff with black spots over back, sides and tail; back of ear black with white spot. Inhabits forest, scrubland and plantations. Usually solitary, but sometimes in pairs or small family groups. Nocturnal, largely terrestrial but can climb trees with ease. Eats mainly small vertebrate animals such as frogs, lizards, birds and rats. In Singapore, present on Pulau Ubin and Pulau Tekong. A roadkill was collected from Mandai Road in 2001 and another from Jalan Bahar in 2007. Distributed from Pakistan, India, China and Indochina, the Philippines, to the Malay Peninsula, Sumatra, Borneo and Java.

Norman Lim

# THREE-STRIPED PALM CIVET or SMALL-TOOTHED PALM CIVET
## *Arctogalidia trivirgata*

Alan Yeo

Carnivora: Viverridae. HB to 52 cm, T to 63 cm. Body long and sleek with short legs, prominent muzzle and a very long tail. Body dark grey usually with three fine black stripes along the back; head, limbs and tail black. Inhabits mature forest. This nocturnal, omnivorous and generally solitary animal is primarily arboreal. In Singapore, apparently confined to the Central Nature Reserves. Distributed over Southeast Asia from Assam, south China and Indochina to the Malay Peninsula, Sumatra and Borneo.

# COMMON PALM CIVET or TODDY CAT
## *Paradoxurus hermaphroditus*

Norman Lim

Carnivora: Viverridae. HB 59 cm, T to 53.5 cm. Body long and sleek with short legs, prominent muzzle and a long tail. Body dark greyish brown with three fine but broken black stripes along the back, and black spots on the sides of the body. Ears and limbs black, a black band across the eyes and side of the muzzle. Forehead, cheeks and fore part of muzzle whitish. Tail black, with or without a white tip. Largely nocturnal, arboreal and omnivorous. Except for females with young kittens, adults are solitary. Inhabits forest, scrubland, parkland and mangroves. In Singapore widespread and quite common, even in urban areas where it frequents gardens and the roof spaces of buildings. The species is, to some extent, commensal with humans. Distributed in India and Sri Lanka, over continental Southeast Asia, Sumatra, Borneo, Java, Sulawesi and the Philippines.

# SMOOTH OTTER or SMOOTH-COATED OTTER
## *Lutrogale perspicillata* (formerly as *Lutra perspicillata*)

Carnivora: Mustelidae. HB to 75 cm, T to 45 cm. Body long and sleek with short limbs, short muzzle and a long ventrally flattened tail. Upperparts greyish brown, underparts buffy; throat and sides of neck cream. Fur short, smooth and sleek. Digits fully webbed, claws prominent. In Singapore, occurs in coastal habitats, largely in mangroves and mudflats. Associates mainly in pairs or small families, and is diurnal in habit. Diet consists mainly of fish. The local population may not be strictly resident for individuals can easily travel between the two shores of the Johor Straits. Regularly seen at Sungei Buloh Wetland Reserve and Pulau Ubin. Also reported from the Western Catchment Area. Distributed from southern Iraq, Pakistan, across India, south China and Indochina, to the Malay Peninsula, Sumatra, Borneo and Java.

Alan Yeo

Fong Chee Wai

# ORIENTAL SMALL-CLAWED OTTER
*Aonyx cinerea* (formerly as *Amblonyx cinereus*)

Carnivora: Mustelidae. HB to 50 cm, T to 33 cm. Body relatively long and sleek with short limbs, short muzzle and a long tail. Upperparts dark brown, paler below; chin, throat, cheeks and sides of neck yellowish. Digits partially webbed; claws short, not extending beyond end of digits. This creature can be active both night and day, and eats mainly crustaceans and molluscs. In Singapore, occurs in small family groups mainly in mangroves and mudflats along the western and northern coast of Singapore Island, particularly in coastal parts of the Western Catchment Area, Sungei Buloh Wetland Reserve and Kranji. Also occurs in Pulau Ubin and Pulau Tekong, and some-times recorded from the reservoirs within the Central Catch-ment Nature Reserve. Distributed from India and south China to the Malay Peninsula, Sumatra, Borneo, Java and Palawan.

Norman Lim

E V E N - T O E D    H O O F E D    M A M M A L S

# WILD PIG or WILD BOAR
*Sus scrofa*

Artiodactyla: Suidae. HB to 1.5 m, T to 30 cm. Body robust, barrel-shaped with large head, relatively slender limbs and a slim tufted tail. Each foot with two main hooves and a small-er lateral hoof. A crest of stiff hairs along the middle of the back. Muzzle long and ending in a truncated nose. Mature animals with long canine teeth (tusks). Generally dark greyish-brown, infants are brown with white stripes. Terrestrial, omnivorous, gregarious and active both day and night. The wild pig inhabits forest, scrubland and mangroves where it digs the soil for roots and worms. Currently the largest resident land mammal in Singapore, the wild pig is found on Pulau Ubin, Pulau Tekong, and in the Western Catchment Area. It is also recorded from wooded areas in Changi, Lim Chu Kang and the Central Catchment Nature Reserve. Once believed to be locally extinct, Singapore was repopulated by individu-als swimming across the Johor Straits from Malaysia. This ancestor of our domestic pig is widely distributed throughout Eurasia.

Benjamin Y. H. Lee

# LESSER MOUSEDEER
*Tragulus kanchil* (formerly confused with *Tragulus javanicus*)

Artiodactyla: Tragulidae. HB to 48 cm, T 9 cm. Body robust, oval-shaped in side view, with a short tail and very slender limbs. Each foot with four toes and two main hooves. Upper-parts reddish brown, centre of nape usually darker. Three white stripes on the underside of the neck. Males with a pair of long canine teeth protruding from upper jaw, but no antlers. Crepuscular and generally solitary but sometimes in pairs. Inhabits mature forest where it is terrestrial and feeds on leaves, shoots, fungi and fallen fruit. In Singapore, restricted to the Central Nature Reserves. Distributed from Indochina through the Malay Peninsula, Sumatra and Borneo.

Chan Kwok Wai

# CHECKLIST

**A checklist of the freshwater fishes, amphibians, terrestrial reptiles and terrestrial mammals of Singapore**

This list covers all species of freshwater fishes (only those that complete their life cycle in freshwater), amphibians, terrestrial reptiles and terrestrial mammals that have been recorded from within the political boundaries of the Republic of Singapore.

For reptiles and mammals, we include species that live in water but do venture onto land from time to time (e.g., water-snakes), as well as those that fly (bats). Marine reptiles (e.g. sea-snakes and marine turtles) and mammals (dolphins and dugongs) are excluded. The predominantly marine Amphibious Sea-snake (*Laticauda colubrina*) is included because it leaves the water deliberately, not just to lay eggs.

As for introduced species, we include only those that are confirmed to be reproducing in large numbers in the feral state. An exception is made for the Red-eared Slider (*Trachemys scripta elegans*), Chinese Softshell Turtle (*Pelodiscus sinensis*) and the American Bullfrog (*Lithobates catesbeianus*). These species probably do not reproduce well in the wild, but are frequently released by the public as unwanted pets or as religious offerings. Humans and domesticated animals (e.g. dog and cat) are excluded.

We have tried to introduce the latest classification and technical names on this list. The reader will find many names unfamiliar and different from those in previous publications. Names used in previous publications (regardless of misidentification or nomenclatural changes) are appended in [ ]. Species illustrated and described in this book are highlighted in bold print.

## Status

The checklist is divided into four parts:

**1) extant indigenous species,**

**2) introduced species,**

**3) extinct species,** and

**4) doubtful/indeterminate species**.

**wc** – widespread and common.

**wu** – widespread but uncommon.

**wr** – widespread but rare.

**rc** – restricted to a few areas but common.

**ru** – restricted to a few areas and uncommon.

**rr** – restricted to a few areas and rare.

**ex** – extinct. Certainly present in the past, and not seen for the last 50 years.

**df** – of doubtful occurrence. Unlikely to have occurred in Singapore because of unsuitable habitat, or because records are based on specimens presumably brought into Singapore by trade.

**vt** – visitor.

**nd** – indeterminate, certainly present in the past but not recorded at least for the past 10 years or more. Not confirmed extinct as their presence may be overlooked due to their small size and/or secretive nature.

# Freshwater Fishes

order CYPRINIFORMES (carps and relatives)
    family Cyprinidae (carps and relatives)
        *Boraras maculatus* (Malayan Pygmy Rasbora) [*Rasbora maculata*] rr
        ***Cyclocheilichthys apogon* (Barbel-less Chemperas)** ru
        ***Rasbora einthovenii* (Einthoven's Rasbora)** rc
        ***Rasbora elegans* (Two-spot Rasbora)** rc
        ***Systomus banksi* (Saddle Barb)** [*Puntius binotatus* in part] rc
        *Systomus hexazona* (Six-banded Tiger Barb) [*Puntius hexazona, Puntius johorensis*] rc
        ***Systomus lateristriga* (T-barb, Spanner Barb)** [*Puntius lateristriga*] rr
        ***Trigonostigma heteromorpha* (Harlequin Rasbora)** [*Rasbora heteromorpha*] rc
    family Nemacheilidae (nemacheilid loaches) [Balitoridae]
        ***Nemacheilus selangoricus* (Grey-banded Sand Loach)** rr
    family Cobitidae (spined loaches)
        ***Pangio muraeniformis* (Spotted Eel-loach)** [*Acanthophthalmus muraeniformis*] rr

order SILURIFORMES (catfishes)
    family Bagridae (Old World river catfishes)
        *Pseudomystus leiacanthus* (Dwarf Bumblebee Catfish) rr
    family Siluridae (sheat catfishes)
        ***Silurichthys hasseltii* (Hasselt's Leaf Catfish)** rr
    family Akysidae (warty catfishes)
        *Parakysis longirostris* (Singapore Little Warty Catfish) [*Parakysis verrucosa*] rr
    family Clariidae (walking catfishes)
        ***Clarias batrachus* (Common Walking Catfish)** wc
        ***Clarias leiacanthus* (Forest Walking Catfish)** [*Clarias teijsmanni*] rr
        ***Clarias nieuhofii* (Slender Walking Catfish)** rr

order BELONIFORMES (garfishes and halfbeaks)
    family Hemiramphidae (halfbeaks)
        ***Dermogenys collettei* (Malayan Pygmy Halfbeak)** [*Dermogenys pusillus*] wc
        ***Hemirhamphodon pogonognathus* (Malayan Forest Halfbeak)** rc

order CYPRINODONTIFORMES (toothcarps)
    family Aplocheilidae (rivulines)
        ***Aplocheilus panchax* (Whitespot)** wc

order SYNBRANCHIFORMES (swamp eels and relatives)
    family Synbranchidae (swamp eels)
        ***Monopterus albus* (Oriental Swamp Eel)** [*Fluta alba*] wc
    family Mastacembelidae (spiny-eels)
        *Macrognathus maculatus* (Buff-backed Spiny-eel) rr

order PERCIFORMES (perches and relatives)
   family Nandidae (leaf-fishes)
      ***Nandus nebulosus* (Sunda Leaf-fish)** rr
   family Eleotridae (gudgeons)
      ***Oxyeleotris marmorata* (Soon Hock, Marbled Gudgeon)** wc
   family Gobiidae (gobies)
      *Gobiopterus brachypterus* (Glass Goby) wc
   family Anabantidae (climbing perches)
      ***Anabas testudineus* (Asian Climbing Perch)** wc
   family Osphronemidae (goramies and fighting-fishes)
      *Betta imbellis* (Crescent Fighting-fish, Paddyfield Fighting-fish) [*Betta splendens*] rr
      ***Betta pugnax* (Malayan Forest Betta)** rc
      ***Luciocephalus pulcher* (Malayan Pikehead)** rr
      ***Trichogaster trichopterus* (Three-spot Goramy, Sepat)** wc
      ***Trichopsis vittata* (Croaking Goramy)** wu
   family Channidae (snakeheads)
      ***Channa gachua* (Dwarf Snakehead)** rr
      ***Channa lucius* (Forest Snakehead, Bujuk)** rr
      ***Channa melasoma* (Black Snakehead)** rr
      ***Channa striata* (Aruan, Common Snakehead)** wc

# Amphibians

order GYMNOPHIONA (caecilians)
   family Ichthyophiidae (Oriental caecilians)
      *Ichthyophis paucisulcus* (Sumatran Striped Caecilian) rr

order ANURA (frogs and toads)
   family Bufonidae (toads)
      ***Duttaphrynus melanostictus* (Asian Toad)** [*Bufo melanostictus*] wc
      ***Ingerophrynus quadriporcatus* (Four-ridged Toad)** [*Bufo quadriporcatus*] rc
      *Pelophryne signata* (Saint Andrew's Cross Toadlet) [*Pelophryne brevipes*] rr
   family Megophryidae (Litter Frogs and relatives)
      ***Leptobrachium nigrops* (Black-eyed Litter Frog)** rc
      ***Megophrys nasuta* (Malayan Horned Frog)** ru
   family Dicroglossidae (fanged frogs and relatives) [Ranidae]
      ***Fejervarya cancrivora* (Crab-eating Frog, Mangrove Frog)** [*Rana cancrivora*] wc
      ***Fejervarya limnocharis* (Field Frog, Grass Frog)** [*Rana limnocharis*] wc
      ***Limnonectes blythii* (Malayan Giant Frog)** [*Rana blythii, Rana macrodon* in part] rc
      ***Limnonectes malesianus* (Malesian Frog)** [*Rana macrodon* in part] rc
      ***Limnonectes paramacrodon* (Masked Swamp Frog)** [*Rana paramacrodon*] rr
      ***Limnonectes plicatellus* (Rhinoceros Frog)** [*Rana plicatella*] rr
      ***Occidozyga sumatrana* (Yellow-bellied Puddle Frog)** [*Occidozyga laevis, Phrynoglossus laevis*] rc
   family Ranidae ('true' frogs)
      ***Hylarana erythraea* (Green Paddy Frog, Common Greenback)** [*Rana erythraea*] wc
      ***Hydrophylax raniceps* (Copper-cheeked Frog, Forest Greenback)** [*Rana chalconota*] rc

**Pulchrana baramica (Golden-eared Rough-sided Frog)** [*Rana baramica*] rr
**Pulchrana laterimaculata (Masked Rough-sided Frog)** [*Rana laterimaculata, Rana baramica*] ru
family Rhacophoridae (gliding frogs and relatives)
**Nyctixalus pictus (Spotted Tree Frog, Cinnamon Bush Frog)** [*Philautus pictus*] rr
**Polypedates leucomystax (Four-lined Tree Frog, Common Tree Frog)**
[*Rhacophorus leucomystax*] wc
**Rhacophorus cyanopunctatus (Blue-legged Bush Frog)** [*Philautus bimaculatus*] rr
**Theloderma horridum (Thorny Bush Frog)** rr
family Microhylidae (narrow-mouthed frogs)
**Kalophrynus pleurostigma (Black-spotted Sticky Frog)** ru
**Microhyla butleri (Painted Chorus Frog)** wc
**Microhyla heymonsi (Dark-sided Chorus Frog)** wc
**Microhyla mantheyi (Manthey's Chorus Frog)** [*Microhyla borneensis*] rr

# Reptiles

order TESTUDINES (turtles and tortoises)
family Geoemydidae  (Asian terrapins) [Bataguridae, Emydidae]
**Cuora amboinensis (Malayan Box Terrapin)** rc
**Cyclemys dentata (Asian Leaf Terrapin)** rr
**Heosemys spinosa (Spiny Hill Terrapin, Spiny Terrapin)** [*Geoemyda spinosa*] rr
**Notochelys platynota (Malayan Flatshell Terrapin)** rr
family Trionychidae (softshell turtles)
**Amyda cartilaginea (Asian Softshell Turtle)** [*Trionyx cartilagineus*] ru
**Dogania subplana (Malayan Forest Softshell Turtle)** rr

order CROCODYLIA (crocodilians)
family Crocodylidae (crocodiles)
**Crocodylus porosus (Estuarine Crocodile, Saltwater Crocodile)** wr

order SQUAMATA  (lizards and snakes)
family Agamidae (dragon-lizards)
**Aphaniotis fusca (Earless Agamid)** rr
**Bronchocela cristatella (Green Crested Lizard)** [*Calotes cristatellus*] wu
**Draco melanopogon (Black-bearded Flying Dragon)** ru
**Draco quinquefasciatus (Five-banded Flying Dragon)** rr
**Draco sumatranus (Sumatran Flying Dragon, Common Flying Dragon)**
[Draco volans] wc
family Eublepharidae (eyelid geckos) [Gekkonidae]
*Aeluroscalabotes felinus* (Fox-faced Gecko) rr
family Gekkonidae (geckos)
**Cnemaspis kendallii (Kendall's Rock Gecko)** [*Gonatodes kendallii*] ru
**Cosymbotus craspedotus (Frilly Gecko)** rr
**Cosymbotus platyurus (Flat-tailed Gecko)** wc
**Cyrtodactylus consobrinus (Peter's Bent-toed Gecko)** rr
**Cyrtodactylus quadrivirgatus (Malayan Marbled Bent-toed Gecko)**
[*Gymnodactylus marmoratus*] ru

# CHECKLIST

  ***Gehyra mutilata* (Four-clawed Gecko)** wc
  *Gekko gecko* (Tokay) rr
  ***Gekko monarchus* (Spotted House Gecko)** wc
  *Gekko smithii* (Stentor Gecko, Large Forest Gecko) [Gekko stentor] rr
  ***Hemidactylus frenatus* (Spiny-tailed House Gecko, Common House Gecko)** wc
  ***Hemiphyllodactylus typus* (Lowland Dwarf Gecko)** rr
  ***Lepidodactylus lugubris* (Maritime Gecko, Mourning Gecko)** wr
  ***Luperosaurus browni* (Brown's Flap-legged Gecko)** rr
  ***Ptychozoon kuhli* (Kuhl's Gliding Gecko)** rr
family Scincidae (skinks)
  ***Dasia grisea* (Brown Tree Skink)** rr
  ***Dasia olivacea* (Olive Tree Skink)** rr
  ***Emoia atrocostata* (Mangrove Skink)** [*Lygosoma atrocostata*] rr
  ***Eutropis multifasciatus* (Many-lined Sun Skink, Common Sun Skink)**
  [*Mabuya multifasciata*] wc
  ***Eutropis rugiferus* (Striped Sun Skink, Rough-scaled Skink)** [*Mabuya rugifera*] rr
  ***Lipinia vittigera* (Striped Tree Skink)** rr
  ***Lygosoma bowringii* (Garden Supple Skink)** [*Riopa bowringii*] wc
  *Sphenomorphus* sp. (Malayan Swamp Skink) rr
family Varanidae (monitors)
  *Varanus dumerili* (Harlequiun Monitor) rr
  ***Varanus nebulosus* (Clouded Monitor)** [*Varanus bengalensis nebulosus*] rc
  ***Varanus salvator* (Malayan Water Monitor)** wc
family Typhlopidae (blind snakes)
  ***Ramphotyphlops braminus* (Brahminy Blind Snake)** [*Typhlops braminus*] wc
  ***Typhlops muelleri* (White-bellied Blind Snake)** [*Typhlops diardi muelleri*] wr
family Cylindrophiidae (Asian pipe snakes)
  *Cylindrophis ruffus* (Red-tailed Pipe Snake) [*Cylindrphis rufus*] wr
family Xenopeltidae (sunbeam snakes)
  ***Xenopeltis unicolor* (Sunbeam Snake, Iridescent Earth Snake)** wu
family Pythonidae (pythons)
  ***Python reticulatus* (Reticulated Python)** wc
family Acrochordidae (file snakes)
  ***Acrochordus granulatus* (Banded File Snake)** [*Chersydrus granulatus*] wc
family Colubridae (colubrid snakes)
  *Ahaetulla fasciolata* (Speckle-headed Whip Snake) rr
  ***Ahaetulla mycterizans* (Malayan Whip Snake, Bigeye Green Whip Snake)** rr
  ***Ahaetulla prasina* (Oriental Whip Snake)** [*Dryophis prasinus*] wc
  ***Boiga cynodon* (Dog-toothed Cat Snake)** rr
  ***Boiga dendrophila* (Gold-ringed Cat Snake, Mangrove Snake)** wr
  ***Boiga jaspidea* (Jasper Cat Snake)** rr
  ***Calamaria lumbricoidea* (Variable Reed Snake)** rr
  ***Calamaria schlegeli* (Pink-headed Reed Snake)** rr
  ***Chrysopelea paradisi* (Paradise Gliding Snake)** [*Chrysopelea ornata*] wc
  ***Chrysopelea pelias* (Twin-barred Gliding Snake)** rr
  ***Coelognathus flavolineatus* (Common Malayan Racer)** [*Elaphe flavolineata*] wr
  ***Dendrelaphis caudolineatus* (Striped Bronzeback)** wc
  ***Dendrelaphis formosus* (Elegant Bronzeback)** [*Dendrelaphis cyanochloris*] rr

***Dendrelaphis kopsteini*** **(Red-necked Bronzeback)** [*Dendrelaphis formosus*] wr
***Dendrelaphis pictus*** **(Painted Bronzeback)** wc
***Dryocalamus subannulatus*** **(Malayan Bridle Snake, Saddled Tree Snake)** rr
***Dryophiops rubescens*** **(Keel-bellied Whip Snake)** rr
***Gongylosoma baliodeirum*** **(Orange-bellied Ringneck)** [*Liopeltis baliodeira*] rr
***Gonyosoma oxycephalum*** **(Red-tailed Racer)** [*Elaphe oxycephala*] rr
***Lycodon capucinus*** **(House Wolf Snake)** [*Ophites capucinus, Lycodon aulicus*] wc
***Lycodon subcinctus*** **(Banded Wolf Snake)** rr
***Oligodon octolineatus*** **(Striped Kukri Snake)** wc
***Oligodon purpurascens*** **(Brown Kukri Snake)** rr
*Oligodon signatus* (Barred Kukri Snake) rr
***Pseudorabdion longiceps*** **(Dwarf Reed Snake)** wr
***Ptyas carinata*** **(Keeled Rat Snake)** [*Zaocys carinatus*] rc
***Ptyas fusca*** **(White-bellied Rat Snake)** [*Zaocys fuscus*] rr
*Ptyas korros* (Indochinese Rat Snake) wu
***Sibynophis melanocephalus*** **(Black-headed Collared Snake)** rr
***Xenelaphis hexagonotus*** **(Malayan Brown Snake)** rr
family Homalopsidae (mud snakes) [Colubridae]
***Cantoria violacea*** **(Cantor's Water Snake)** wr
***Cerberus rynchops*** **(Dog-faced Water Snake)** wc
***Fordonia leucobalia*** **(Crab-eating Water Snake)** wr
***Gerarda prevostiana*** **(Yellow-lipped Water Snake)** wr
***Homalopsis buccata*** **(Puff-faced Water Snake)** wu
family Natricidae (keelbacks) [Colubridae]
***Macropisthodon rhodomelas*** **(Blue-necked Keelback)** wr
***Psammodynastes pictus*** **(Painted Mock Viper)** rr
***Xenochrophis maculatus*** **(Spotted Keelback)** [*Natrix maculata*] ru
*Xenochrophis trianguligerus* (Triangle Keelback) [*Natrix trianguligera*] rr
family Elapidae (cobras, coral-snakes, sea-snakes)
***Bungarus fasciatus*** **(Banded Krait)** rr
***Calliophis bivirgatus*** **(Blue Malayan Coral Snake)** [*Maticora bivirgata*] rr
***Calliophis intestinalis*** **(Banded Malayan Coral Snake)** [*Maticora intestinalis*] wr
***Naja sumatrana*** **(Equatorial Spitting Cobra, Black Spitting Cobra)** [*Naja naja*] wc
***Ophiophagus hannah*** **(King Cobra)** [*Naja hannah*] rr
family Hydrophiidae (sea-snakes)
***Laticauda colubrina*** **(Yellow-lipped Sea Krait, Amphibious Sea Snake)** wc
family Viperidae (vipers) [Crotalidae]
***Cryptelytrops purpureomaculatus*** **(Mangrove Pit-viper, Shore Pit-viper)**
[*Trimeresurus purpureomaculatus*] rr
***Tropidolaemus wagleri*** **(Wagler's Pit-viper)** [*Trimeresurus wagleri*] rr

# Mammals

order SCANDENTIA (treeshrews)
    family Tupaiidae (treeshrews)
        ***Tupaia glis* (Common Treeshrew)** wc

order DERMOPTERA (flying lemurs or colugos)
    family Cynocephalidae (colugos)
        ***Galeopterus variegatus* (Malayan Colugo, Malayan Flying Lemur)**
        [*Cynocephalus variegatus*] rc

order PRIMATES (primates)
    family Lorisidae (lorises)
        ***Nycticebus coucang* (Sunda Slow Loris)** rr
    family Cercopithecidae (Old World monkeys)
        ***Macaca fascicularis* (Long-tailed Macaque, Crab-eating Macaque)** wc
        ***Presbytis femoralis* (Banded Leaf Monkey, Banded Langur)**
        [*Presbytis melalophos*] rr

order RODENTIA (rodents)
    family Sciuridae (squirrels)
        ***Callosciurus notatus* (Plantain Squirrel)** wc
        ***Hylopetes spadiceus* (Red-cheeked Flying Squirrel)** rr
        ***Iomys horsfieldii* (Horsfield's Flying Squirrel)** rr
        *Rhinosciurus laticaudatus* (Shrew-faced Ground Squirrel) rr
        ***Sundasciurus tenuis* (Slender Squirrel)** rc
    family Muridae (rats and mice)
        ***Maxomys rajah* (Brown Spiny Rat, Rajah Spiny Rat)** rr
        ***Mus musculus* (House Mouse)** [*Mus castaneus*] wc
        ***Rattus annandalei* (Annandale's Rat, Singapore Rat)** rc
        *Rattus exulans* (Polynesian Rat, Little Burmese Rat) wu
        ***Rattus rattus* (House Rat)** wc
        ***Rattus tiomanicus* (Malaysian Wood Rat)** wc
    family Hystricidae (Old World porcupines)
        ***Hystrix brachyura* (Malayan Porcupine)** rr

order SORICOMORPHA (shrews and relatives)
    family Soricidae (shrews)
        ***Suncus murinus* (House Shrew)** wc
        *Crocidura fuliginosa* (Southeast Asian White-toothed Shrew) rr – pending a
        detailed study, the Singapore population may be referred to *Crocidura malayana*.

order CHIROPTERA (bats)
    family Pteropodidae (Old World fruit bats)
        ***Cynopterus brachyotis* (Lesser Dog-faced Fruit Bat, Common Fruit Bat)** wc
        *Cynopterus sphinx* (Short-nosed Fruit Bat) rr
        ***Eonycteris spelaea* (Cave Nectar Bat)** wu
        *Macroglossus minimus* (Common Long-tongued Nectar Bat) rr

*Penthetor lucasi* **(Dusky Fruit Bat)** rr
*Pteropus vampyrus* (Large Flying Fox) vt
family Rhinolophidae (horseshoe bats)
**Rhinolophus lepidus (Glossy Horseshoe Bat, Blyth's Horseshoe Bat)**
[*Rhinolophus refulgens*] rc
*Rhinolophus luctus* (Great Woolly Horseshoe Bat) rr
**Rhinolophus trifoliatus (Trefoil Horseshoe Bat)** rr
family Megadermatidae (false vampires)
**Megaderma spasma (Lesser False Vampire, Malayan False Vampire)** rr
family Emballonuridae (sheath-tailed bats)
*Emballonura monticola* (Lesser Sheath-tailed Bat) rr
**Saccolaimus saccolaimus (Pouch-bearing Bat)** [*Taphozous saccolaimus*] wc
*Taphozous melanopogon* (Black-bearded Tomb Bat) wr
family Nycteridae (hollow-faced bats)
*Nycteris tragata* (Southeast Asian Hollow-faced Bat) rr
family Molossidae (free-tailed bats)
*Cheiromeles torquatus* (Naked Bulldog Bat) rr
family Vespertilionidae (evening bats)
*Kerivoula* sp. (Woolly Bat) rr
*Murina suilla* (Brown Tube-nosed Bat) rr
**Myotis muricola (Whiskered Myotis)** [*Myotis mystacina*] wc
**Myotis adversus (Grey Large-footed Myotis)** wc
**Scotophilus kuhlii (Lesser Asiatic Yellow House Bat)** wc
**Tylonycteris pachypus (Lesser Bamboo Bat)** rr
**Tylonycteris robustula (Greater Bamboo Bat)** wc

order PHOLIDOTA (pangolins)
family Manidae (pangolins)
**Manis javanica (Sunda Pangolin, Malayan Scaly Anteater)** wr

order CARNIVORA (carnivores)
family Felidae (cats)
**Prionailurus bengalensis (Leopard Cat)** [*Felis bengalensis*] rr
family Viverridae (civets)
**Arctogalidia trivirgata (Three-striped Palm Civet, Small-toothed Palm Civet)** rr
*Paguma larvata* (Masked Palm Civet) rr?
**Paradoxurus hermaphroditus (Common Palm Civet, Toddy Cat)** wu
family Mustelidae (weasels and relatives)
**Lutrogale perspicillata (Smooth Otter, Smooth-coated Otter)** [*Lutra perspicillata*] wr
**Aonyx cinerea (Oriental Small-clawed Otter)** [*Amblonyx cinereus*] rr

order ARTIODACTYLA (even-toed hoofed mammals)
family Suidae (pigs)
**Sus scrofa (Wild Pig, Wild Boar)** rc
family Tragulidae (mouse-deer, chevrotains)
**Tragulus kanchil (Lesser Mousedeer)** [*Tragulus javanicus*] rr

# INTRODUCED SPECIES

## Freshwater Fishes

order RAJIFORMES (rays and skates)
    family Potamotrygonidae (South American river stingrays)
        *Potamotrygon motoro* (Motoro Ray) rr

order OSTEOGLOSSIFORMES (bony-tongues and relatives)
    family Osteoglossidae (bony-tongues)
        *Scleropages formosus* (Asian Arowana) wr
    family Notopteridae (Old World knife-fishes)
        *Chitala ornata* (Clown Featherback) rc
        *Notopterus notopterus* (Black Featherback) rc

order CYPRINIFORMES (carps and relatives)
    family Cyprinidae  (carps and relatives)
        *Barbonymus schwanenfeldii* (Stripe-tailed Tinfoil Barb) [*Barbodes schwanenfeldii*] rc
        *Esomus metallicus* (Siamese Flying Barb) rr
        *Hampala macrolepidota* (Sebarau) rc
        *Metzia lineata* (Chinese Minnow) [*Rasborinus lineatus, Rasborichthys altior*] nd
        *Osteochilus hasselti* (Terbol, Hasselt's Bony-lipped Barb) rc
        *Puntius semifasciolatus* (Green Barb) rr
        *Rasbora borapetensis* (Red-tailed Rasbora) wc
        *Systomus partipentazona* (Indochinese Tiger Barb) [*Puntius partipentazona*] wc
        *Systomus rhombeus* (Indochinese Spotted Barb) [*Puntius binotatus* in part] rc
        *Systomus tetrazona* (Sumatran Tiger Barb) wc

order SILURIFORMES (catfishes)
    family Clariidae (walking catfishes)
        *Clarias gariepinus* (African Walking Catfish) wc
    family Loricariidae (armoured sucking catfishes)
        *Pterygoplichthys disjunctivus* (Marbled-belly Armoured Sucking Catfish)
        [*Hypostomus* sp. in part] wr?
        *Pterygoplichthys pardalis* (Spotted-belly Armoured Sucking Catfish)
        [*Liposarcus pardalis, Hypostomus* sp. in part] wc

order CYPRINODONTIFORMES (toothcarps)
    family Poeciliidae (live-bearing toothcarps)
        *Gambusia affinis* (Mosquitofish) [*Gambusia holbrookii*] wc
        **Poecilia reticulata (Guppy)** [*Lebistes reticulatus*] wc

order SYNBRANCHIFORMES (swamp eels and relatives)
    family Mastacembelidae (spiny-eels)
        *Macrognathus zebrinus* (Zebra Spiny-eel) rc

order PERCIFORMES (perches and relatives)
    family Ambassidae (glass-perches)
        *Parambassis siamensis* (Indochinese Glass-perchlet) [*Chanda* sp.] wc
    family Cichlidae (cichlids)
        *Acarichthys heckelli* (Threadfin Acara) wc
        *Cichla orinocensis* (Peacock Bass) wc
        *Cichlasoma urophthalmus* (Mayan Cichlid) wc
        *Cichlasoma* hybrid (Luohan) wc
        *Geophagus altifrons* (Eartheater) wc
        ***Oreochromis mossambicus* (Mozambique Tilapia)** [*Tilapia mossambica*] wc
        *Parachromis managuensis* (Jaguar Guapote) rc
        *Paratheraps synspilus* (Red-breasted Cichlid) rc
        *Tilapia buttikoferi* (Hornet Tilapia) wc
    family Gobiidae (gobies)
        *Rhinogobius giurinus* (East Asian River Goby) [*Stigmatogobius poecilosoma*] wc
    family Osphronemidae (goramies and fighting-fishes)
        *Osphronemus goramy* (Common Giant Goramy, Kalui) wc
        *Trichogaster pectoralis* (Snakeskin Goramy, Sepat Siam) rr
    family Channidae (snakeheads)
        ***Channa micropeltes* (Toman, Giant Snakehead)** wc

# Amphibians

order ANURA (frogs and toads)
    family Microhylidae (narrow-mouthed frogs)
        ***Kaloula pulchra* (Banded Bull Frog)** wc
        ***Microhyla fissipes* (East Asian Ornate Chorus Frog)** [*Microhyla ornata*] rr
    family Ranidae ('true' frogs)
        *Lithobates catesbeianus* (American Bullfrog) [*Rana catesbeiana*] wc

# Reptiles

order TESTUDINES (turtles and tortoises)
    family Geoemydidae  (Asian terrapins) [Bataguridae, Emydidae]
        ***Siebenrockiella crassicollis* (Black Marsh Terrapin)** wc
    family Emydidae  (American terrapins)
        ***Trachemys scripta elegans* (Red-eared Slider, Elegant Slider)** [*Pseudemys scripta elegans*] wc
    family Trionychidae (softshell turtles)
        ***Pelodiscus sinensis* (Chinese Softshell Turtle)** [*Trionyx sinensis*] wc

order SQUAMATA  (lizards and snakes)
    family Agamidae (dragon-lizards)
        ***Calotes versicolor* (Changeable Lizard)** wc
    family Pareatidae (slug-eating snakes) [Colubridae]
        ***Pareas margaritophorus* (White-spotted Slug Snake)** wc

family Natricidae (keelbacks)
    *Xenochrophis flavipunctatus* (Indochinese Chequered Keelback)
    [*Xenochrophis piscator, Natrix piscator*] rr
    ***Xenochrophis vittatus* (Striped Keelback)** wc

# Mammals

order RODENTIA (rodents)
    family Sciuridae (squirrels)
        ***Callosciurus finlaysonii* (Variable Squirrel)** rc
    family Muridae (rats and mice)
        ***Rattus norvegicus* (Brown Rat)** wc

# EXTINCT SPECIES
## Freshwater Species

order CYPRINIFORMES (carps and relatives)
    family Cyprinidae  (carps and relatives)
        *Osteochilus spilurus* (Swamp Bony-lipped Barb) ex
        *Rasbora cephalotaenia* (Head-banded Rasbora) ex
        *Systomus dunckeri* (Malayan Clown Barb) [*Puntius dunckeri*] ex

order SILURIFORMES (catfishes)
    family Siluridae (sheat catfishes)
        *Ompok fumidus* (Smokey Ompok) ex
    family Clariidae (walking catfishes)
        *Clarias meladerma* (Saw-spined Walking Catfish) ex

order PERCIFORMES (perches and relatives)
    family Osphronemidae (goramies and fighting-fishes)
        *Belontia hasselti* (Hasselt's Combtail) ex
        *Betta tomi* (Mawai Giant Fighting-fish) ex

## Reptiles

order SQUAMATA  (lizards and snakes)
    family Pythonidae (pythons)
        *Python brongersmai* (Blood Python, Malayan Short Python) [*Python curtus*] ex

# Mammals

order PRIMATES (primates)
    family Cercopithecidae (Old World monkeys)
        *Macaca nemestrina* (Pig-tailed Macaque) ex

order RODENTIA (rodents)
    family Sciuridae (squirrels)
        *Lariscus insignis* (Three-striped Ground Squirrel) ex
    family Muridae (rats)
        *Maxomys surifer* (Red Spiny Rat) [*Rattus surifer*] ex?

order CARNIVORA (carnivores)
    family Felidae (cats)
        *Panthera pardus* (Leopard, Panther) ex/rr?
        *Panthera tigris* (Tiger) ex
        *Prionailurus planiceps* (Flat-headed Cat) [*Felis planiceps*] ex
    family Viverridae (civets)
        *Arctictis binturong* (Binturong, Bear-cat) ex

order ARTIODACTYLA (even-toed hoofed mammals)
    family Cervidae (deer)
        *Rusa unicolor* (Sambar) ex/in [*Cervus unicolor*]
        *Muntiacus muntjak* (Red Muntjac, Barking Deer) ex

## DOUBTFUL/INDETERMINATE SPECIES
## Freshwater Fishes

order CYPRINIFORMES (carps and relatives)
    family Cyprinidae (carps and relatives)
        *Discherodontus halei* (Malayan Spot-finned Barb) df
        *Labiobarbus festivus* (Stripe-tailed Kawan) df
        *Osteochilus melanopleurus* (Kelabau) df
        *Oxygaster anomalura* (Keel-bellied Minnow) df
        *Rasbora gracilis* (Slender Rasbora) df
        *Rasbora paucisqualis* (Silver Rasbora) [*Rasbora bankanensis*] nd – last recorded in 1963.
        *Tor tambroides* (Long-lipped Kelah, Malayan Mahseer) df
    family Cobitidae (spined loaches)
        *Pangio semicincta* (Malayan Banded Eel-loach) [*Pangio kuhlii*] nd – last recorded in 1963.

order SILURIFORMES (catfishes)
    family Bagridae (Old World river catfishes)
        *Hemibagrus nemurus* (Black-lined Baung) [*Mystus nemurus*] df
    family Siluridae (sheat catfishes)
        *Kryptopterus micronemus* (Short-whiskered Sheat Catfish) df

*Ompok bimaculatus* (Two-spotted Ompok) df
*Wallago leerii* (Tapah) df
family Sisoridae (sisorid catfishes)
*Glyptothorax fuscus* (Indochinese Wrinkle-bellied Catfish) [*Glyptothorax major*] nd
– last recorded in 1963.

order SYNBRANCHIFORMES (swamp eels and relatives)
family Mastacembelidae (spiny-eels)
*Macrognathus tapirus* (Largenose Spiny-eel) [*Macrognathus aculeatus*] df
*Mastacembelus favus* (Tyretrack Spiny-eel) df

order PERCIFORMES (perches and relatives)
family Pristolepididae (maroon perches)
*Pristolepis fasciata* (Banded Maroon Perch) df

# Amphibians

order GYMNOPHIONA (caecilians)
family Ichthyophiidae (Oriental caecilians)
*Ichthyophis singaporensis* (Singapore Black Caecilian) nd

order ANURA (frogs and toads)
family Dicroglossidae (fanged frogs and relatives) [Ranidae]
*Limnonectes doriae* (Doria's Frog) [*Rana doriae*] df

# Reptiles

order TESTUDINES (turtles and tortoises)
family Geoemydidae (Asian terrapins)
*Callagur borneoensis* (Painted Terrapin) nd
family Trionychidae (softshell turtles)
*Pelochelys cantorii* (Asian Giant Softshell Turtle) [*Pelochelys bibroni*] nd

order CROCODYLIA (crocodilians)
family Crocodylidae (crocodiles)
*Crocodylus siamensis* (Siamese Crocodile) df

order SQUAMATA (lizards and snakes)
family Agamidae (dragon-lizards)
*Acanthosaura armata* (Horned Tree Lizard) df
*Draco fimbriatus* (Fimbriate Flying Dragon) nd
*Draco maculatus* (Spotted Flying Dragon) nd
*Gonocephalus bellii* (Bell's Anglehead) [*Goniocephalus borneensis*] df

family Gekkonidae (geckos)
*Cyrtodactylus pulchellus* (Banded Bent-toed Gecko) [*Gymnodactylus pulchellus*] df
*Hemidactylus brookii* (Brooke's House Gecko) nd

*Hemidactylus garnotii* (Garnot's House Gecko) nd
*Ptychozoon horsfieldii* (Horsfield's Gliding Gecko) nd
family Typhlopidae (blind snakes)
*Ramphotyphlops lineatus* (Striped Blind Snake) [*Typhlops lineatus*] nd
family Acrochordidae (file snakes)
*Acrochordus javanicus* (Elephant Trunk Water Snake) df
family Colubridae (colubrid snakes)
*Boiga drapiezii* (White-spotted Cat Snake) nd
*Calamaria albiventer* (Red-bellied Reed Snake) nd
*Calamaria gimletti* (Gimlett's Reed Snake) nd
*Coelognathus radiatus* (Copperhead Racer) [*Elaphe radiata*] nd
*Gonyophis margaritatus* (Rainbow Tree Snake) nd
*Liopeltis tricolor* (Tricoloured Ringneck) nd
*Oreocryptophis porphyraceus* (Red Mountain Racer) [*Elaphe porphyracea*] df
*Orthriophis taeniurus* (Striped Racer, Cave Racer) [*Elaphe taeniura*] nd
*Ptyas mucosa* (Banded Rat Snake) nd
family Homalopsidae (mud snakes) [Colubridae]
*Bitia hydroides* (Keel-bellied Water Snake) nd
*Enhydris enhydris* (Rainbow Water Snake) nd
*Enhydris indica* (Malayan Water Snake) df
family Natricidae (keelbacks) [Colubridae]
*Amphiesma petersii* (Peter's Keelback) [*Natrix petersii*] nd
*Rhabdophis subminiatus* (Red-necked Keelback) [*Natrix subminiata*] nd
family Elapidae (cobras, coral-snakes)
*Bungarus candidus* (Malayan Krait, Blue Krait) nd
*Calliophis gracilis* (Spotted Malayan Coral Snake) nd
family Viperidae (vipers) [Crotalidae]
*Ovophis convictus* (Malayan Mountain Pit-viper) [*Trimeresurus monticola*] df
*Parias hageni* (Hagen's Pit-viper) [*Trimeresurus sumatranus*] nd
*Popeia popeiorum* (Pope's Pit-viper) [*Trimeresurus popeorum*] df

# Mammals

order PROBOSCIDEA (elephants)
family Elephantidae (elephants)
*Elephas maximus* (Asian Elephant) nd/vt – recorded in 1990 (three on Pulau Tekong) and 1991 (one on Pulau Ubin).

order SCANDENTIA (treeshrews)
family Ptilocercidae (pen-tailed treeshrews)
*Ptilocercus lowii* (Pen-tailed Treeshrew) df – see Helgen (in Wilson & Reeder, 2005: 109).

order RODENTIA (rodents)
family Sciuridae (squirrels)
*Callosciurus prevostii* (Prevost's Squirrel) df
*Petaurista petaurista* (Red Giant Flying Squirrel) nd – last recorded in 1986.
*Ratufa affinis* (Cream-coloured Giant Squirrel) nd – last recorded in 1995.

# CHECKLIST

family Spalacidae (bamboo rats and zokors)
*Rhizomys sumatrensis* (Large Bamboo Rat) df

Order ERINACEOMORPHA (hedgehogs)
family Erinaceidae (hedgehogs)
*Echinosorex gymnurus* (Moonrat, Gymnure) df

order CHIROPTERA (bats)
family Pteropodidae (Old World fruit bats)
*Cynopterus horsfieldii* (Larger Dog-faced Fruit Bat) nd
*Rousettus amplexicaudatus* (Geoffroy's Rousette) nd
family Rhinolophidae (horseshoe bats)
*Rhinolophus sedulus* (Lesser Woolly Horseshoe Bat) nd
*Rhinolophus stheno* (Lesser Brown Horseshoe Bat) nd
family Hipposideridae (leaf-nosed bats)
*Hipposideros bicolor* (Bicoloured Leaf-nosed Bat) nd
*Hipposideros cervinus* (Common Leaf-nosed Bat) nd
*Hipposideros ridleyi* (Ridley's Leaf-nosed Bat) nd
family Molossidae (free-tailed bats)
*Chaerephon plicata* (Wrinkle-lipped Free-tailed Bat) [*Tadarida plicata*] nd
family Vespertilionidae (evening bats)
*Myotis oreias* (Singapore Myotis) nd
*Nyctalus noctula* (Noctule) df
*Pipistrellus javanicus* (Javan Pipistrelle) nd
*Pipistrellus stenopterus* (Narrow-winged Pipistrelle) nd

order CARNIVORA (carnivores)
family Felidae (cats)
*Neofelis nebulosa* (Clouded Leopard) df
family Viverridae (civets)
*Cynogale bennettii* (Sunda Otter-civet) df
*Viverra megaspila* (Large-spotted Civet) df
*Viverra tangalunga* (Malay Civet, Sunda Civet) nd
*Viverra zibetha* (Large Indian Civet) nd
*Viverricula indica* (Small Indian Civet, Little Civet) nd
family Herpestidae (mongooses)
*Herpestes brachyurus* (Short-tailed Mongoose) df – see Wozencraft (in Wilson & Reeder, 2005: 567).
family Mustelidae (weasels and relatives)
*Lutra sumatrana* (Hairy-nosed Otter) df

order PERISSODACTYLA (odd-toed hoofed mammals)
family Tapiridae (tapirs)
*Tapirus indicus* (Malayan Tapir) nd/vt – record based on a photograph of a dead individual found in 1986 on Pulau Ubin.

order ARTIODACTYLA (even-toed hoofed mammals)
family Tragulidae (mouse-deer, chevrotains)
*Tragulus napu* (Greater Mousedeer) nd

# REFERENCES AND FURTHER READING

Chou, L. M., H. T. W. Tan & D. C. J. Yeo, 2006. *The Natural Heritage of Singapore*. Pearson/ Prentice Hall, Singapore. vii +244 pages.

Corbet, G. B. & J. E. Hill, 1992. *The Mammals of the Indomalayan Region: a systematic review*. Natural History Museum Publications, Oxford University Press. 488 pages.

Cox, M. J., van Dijk, P. P., Nabhitabhata, J. & K. Thirakhupt. 1998. *A Photographic Guide to Snakes and Other Reptiles of Peninsular Malaysia, Singapore and Thailand*. New Holland Publishers (UK) Ltd. 144 pages.

Das, I., 2004. *Lizards of Borneo*. Natural History Publications (Borneo). vi + 83 pages.

Francis, C. M., 2001. *A Photographic Guide to Mammals of South-east Asia*. New Holland Publishers (UK) Ltd. 128 pages.

Kottelat, M., Whitten, A. J., Kartikasari, S. N. & S. Wirjoatmodjo, 1993. *Freshwater Fishes of Western Indonesia and Sulawesi*. Periplus Editions Ltd. xxxviii + 221 pages, 84 colour plates.

Lim, K. K. P. & F. L. K. Lim, 1992. *A Guide to the Amphibians and Reptiles of Singapore*. Singapore Science Centre. 160 pages.

Lim, K. K. P. & P. K. L. Ng, 1990. *A Guide to the Freshwater Fishes of Singapore*. Singapore Science Centre. 160 pages.

Lim, Norman, 2007. *Colugo: the Flying Lemur of South-east Asia*. Draco Publishing, Singapore. 80 pages.

Manthey, U. & W. Grossmann, 1997. *Amphibien & Reptilien Südostasiens*. Natur und Tier – Verlag. 512 pages.

Medway, Lord, 1983. *The Wild Mammals of Malaya (Peninsular Malaysia) and Singapore*. Second edition reprinted with corrections. Oxford University Press, Kuala Lumpur. xxiii + 131 pages., 15 colour plates.

Nelson, J. S., 2006. *Fishes of the World*. Fourth edition. John Wiley & Sons, Inc. xix + 601 pages.

Ng, P. K. L. (editor), 1995. *A Guide to the Threatened Animals of Singapore*. Singapore Science Centre. 160 pages.

Sigurdsson, J. B. & C. M. Yang, 1990. Marine mammals of Singapore. In: Chou, L. M. & P. K. L. Ng (editors). *Essays in Zoology*. Department of Zoology, National University of Singapore. Page 25-37.

Teo, R. C. H. & R. Subaraj, 1997. Mammals, reptiles and amphibians in the Nature Reserves of Singapore – diversity, abundance and distribution. *The Gardens' Bulletin, Singapore*. 49: 353-425.

Tweedie, M. W. F., 1983. *The Snakes of Malaya*. Third Edition. Singapore National Printers (Pte) Ltd. 167 pages.

Wilson, D. E. & D. M. Reeder (editors), 2005. *Mammal Species of the World: a Taxonomic and Geographic Reference*. Third Edition. Johns Hopkins University Press. 2142 pages in two volumes.

Yang, C. M., Yong, K. & K. K. P. Lim, 1990. Wild mammals of Singapore. In: Chou, L. M. & P. K. L. Ng (editors). *Essays in Zoology*. Department of Zoology, National University of Singapore. Page 1-23.

# GLOSSARY

**Aerial** – moving in the air.

**Amphibious** – spending equal amounts of time in water and on land.

**Anus** – opening at rear end of body through which food wastes are discharged.

**Aquatic** – living entirely in water.

**Arboreal** – living off the ground on elevated surfaces, such as trees.

**Bar / Band** – vertical or transverse elongated patch of colour.

**Barbel** – fleshy hair-like sensory organ usually found around the mouth of certain fishes. Sometimes informally called 'whiskers'.

**Benthic** – living on the ground levels of aquatic environments, such as the seafloor.

**Buffy** – faded yellow colour.

**Bukit** – Malay term for hill.

**Canine teeth** – teeth located at the sides of the jaws at the front, usually long and sharp (fangs), sometimes curved and protruding out of the mouth (tusks).

**Carnivorous** – feeding on animal flesh.

**Caudal peduncle** – region of a fish's body between the tail base and the rear end of the anal fin base.

**Cephalopods** – shell-less molluscs with tentacles that include squids and octopuses.

**Chevron** – 'V'-shaped.

**Cloaca** – opening at rear end of body (of fish, amphibians, reptiles and birds) through which bodily wastes are discharged, sexual organs protrude, and eggs and young are expelled.

**Compressed** – laterally pressed together.

**Commensal** – living in close association.

**Continental Southeast Asia** – the south-eastern corner of the Asian continent comprising the countries of Myanmar, Thailand, Laos, Vietnam, Cambodia, Malaysia and Singapore.

**Crepuscular** – active at dawn and dusk.

**Crustaceans** – a group of invertebrate animals with jointed limbs and hard exoskeletons which comprises the crabs and shrimps.

**Depressed** – dorso-ventrally pressed together.

**Digits** – fingers and toes.

**Diurnal** – active in the day.

**Dorsum** – the back of an animal.

**Endemic** – occurring only in a particular place.

**Estuary** – mouth of a river that opens out into the sea.

**Extant** – still in existence.

**Feral** – referring to introduced organisms that managed to establish self-sustaining populations in the wild.

**Folivorous** – feeding on leaves.

**Fossorial** – living under ground.

**Frugivorous** – feeding on fruits.

**Gonopodium** – a flexible rod-like male organ on certain groups of fish used for transferring sperm to a female.

**Gregarious** – living in groups.

**Herbivorous** – feeding on vegetable matter.

**Hyaline** – transluscent white.

**Incisors** – teeth, usually rectangular in shape, located at the front of the jaws.

**Indian Subcontinent** – the triangular land mass together with Sri Lanka demarcated from the rest of Asia by the Himalayan mountain range in the north.

**Indigenous** – occurring naturally in a particular place.

**Indo-Pacific** – refers to the seas, islands and coastal lands within the Pacific and

Indian oceans, from the east African coast eastwards to the western coastlines of the Americas.

**Indo-west Pacific** – refers to the seas, islands and coasts within the Indian Ocean and the western half of the Pacific Ocean, from the east African coast eastwards to the Hawaiian Islands.

**Insectivorous** – feeding on insects.

**Invertebrate** – an animal without a backbone, e.g. worm, insect, crustacean, scorpion, mollusc.

**Kampung** – Malay term for village.

**Keeled** – with a raised surface that is narrow and sharp.

**Mollusc / Mollusk** – a group of invertebrate animals with soft bodies and often covered with a shell. Includes snails, clams, limpets, slugs and squids.

**Malay Peninsula** – the strip of land that juts out of the southeastern corner of the Asian continent from the Isthmus of Kra. It includes southern Thailand, Peninsular Malaysia and Singapore.

**Mangroves** – a group of trees with aerial root systems found along muddy coasts. Here referring to the habitat dominated by such trees.

**Muzzle** – front part (including the snout) of a mammal's face.

**Nape** – back of the neck behind the head.

**Native** – as per 'indigenous', occurring naturally in a particular place.

**Nocturnal** – active in the night.

**Omnivorous** – feeds on both plant and animal matter.

**Oviparous** – egg laying.

**Parkland** – habitat characterised by artificially trimmed and managed vegetation.

**Parthenogenesis** – mode of reproduction that does not involve the male sex.

**Patagium** – skin membrane attached to the body that aids in gliding.

**Pelagic** – living in the open sea far from shore, or living in midwater.

**Peninsular Malaysia** – the part of the Malay Peninsula and adjacent islands that fall within the political boundaries of Malaysia.

**Piscivorous** – feeds on fish.

**Poaching** – collecting animals and plants illegally and without permission.

**Pulau** – Malay term for island.

**Rural** – environment characterised by agricultural activities.

**Scrubland** – habitat that has been recently cleared, and covered with naturally regenerating vegetation such as long grass, bushes and isolated trees.

**Serrated** – with a row of connected sharp conical shapes.

**Snout** – part of head in front of the eyes (also refers to the long nose of certain mammals).

**Solitary** – living alone.

**Southeast Asia** – includes continental Southeast Asia, the Philippine Islands, Sumatra, Borneo, Java and Sulawesi, and their adjacent islands.

**Stripe** – horizontal or longitudinal elongated patch of colour.

**Sungei** – Malay term for waterway (e.g. stream or river).

**Tadpole** – larval stage of amphibians.

**Terrestrial** – living on the ground.

**Truncate** – as if having the end portion abruptly sliced off.

**Ventrum** – referring to the under surface of animals.

# THE VERTEBRATE STUDY GROUP

The Vertebrate Study Group (VSG) is a special interest group of the Nature Society (Singapore). It was formed in 1993 by a few members with a shared interest in the higher animals – the vertebrates. As birds and marine fish are covered by other special interest groups within the society, the Vertebrate Study Group primarily covers the remaining taxa - mammals, reptiles, amphibians and freshwater fish.

Many members of the VSG committee and their associates are not practising zoologists, but they share a deep interest in animal life and diversity. The primary goal of the group lies in the field studies of vertebrates in Singapore. It firmly believes that to better understand, conserve and protect Singapore's native fauna, up-to-date data is a prerequisite, and the group has, in collaboration with the National Parks Board, the Singapore Ministry of Defence, and the National University of Singapore, been actively recording personal observations and conducting surveys in nature areas all over Singapore.

Committee members of 2007: Subaraj Rajathurai (Chairperson), Celine Low (Secretary), Nick Baker, Chan Kwok Wai, Cheryl Chia, Vilma D'Rozario, Leong Tzi Ming, Kelvin Lim, Norman Lim, Tony O'Dempsey, Timothy Pwee, Robert Teo, Yeo Suay Hwee.

Kelvin Lim

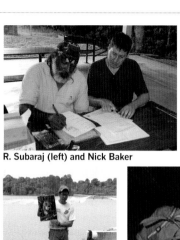
R. Subaraj (left) and Nick Baker

Robert Teo

Leong Tzi Ming

Yeo Suay Hwee

Tony O'Dempsey

Kelvin Lim

Chan Kwok Wai

Norman Lim

Vilma D'Rozario (left) and
Celine Low

Cheryl Chia

Timothy Pwee

# ACKNOWLEDGEMENTS

The Vertebrate Study Group (VSG) is greatly indebted to its sponsor, Aabar Petroleum Investments, for their generous funding. Nick Baker personally thanks Chris Gibson-Robinson, Tanya Pang, Jim Parkin and Richard Lorentz, of the Pearl Energy subsidiary of Aabar, for their support and patient understanding during the production of this long overdue guide.

A big thank you goes to friends of the VSG in the Nature Society (Singapore), too numerous to mention, who help in their own ways – by the submission of sighting records, and by the generous use of images.

The VSG extends its deep thanks as well to friends in the National Parks Board, again too numerous to mention, for their enthusiasm, camaraderie and support over the years. They too were most generous with wildlife images.

The VSG is grateful to the Department of Biological Sciences, National University of Singapore (NUS), for their continuing support and shared enthusiasm for the wildlife of Singapore.

We acknowledge the valuable role played by Singapore's Ministry Of Defence in granting permission to various individuals and groups to take part in wildlife surveys in restricted areas. Without such support the existence of a number of rare vertebrate species would have gone unrecorded.

Kelvin Lim personally thanks Peter K. L. Ng, director of the Raffles Museum of Biodiversity Research of the NUS, Indraneil Das, Maurice Kottelat, Francis Lim and Lim Boo Liat for all the years of guidance.

Nick Baker thanks his supportive wife, Sophia, who is always the first to see his photos of a rare snake or lizard.

Finally, a special mention goes to The Earl of Cranbrook. As a veteran of the study of Southeast Asia's wildlife, the VSG is honoured to have him write his kind foreword.

**PHOTO CREDITS**

This book would not have been possible without photographs taken by the following people:

Alan Yeo, Benjamin Y. H. Lee, Chan Kwok Wai, Celine Low, Chua Siew Chin, Daniel Koh, Derek Liew, Fong Chee Wai, Gloria Seow, Ho Hua Chew, Joe Lim, Tsang Kwok Choong, Kelvin Lim, Lee King Li, Lim Swee Cheng, Leong Tzi Ming, Morten Strange, Nick Baker, Norman Lim, Tony O'Dempsey, Ria Tan, Robert Teo, Shirley Pottie, Tan Heok Hui, Tay Soon Lian, Thiha Zan and Yeo Suay Hwee.

# INDEX

# INDEX